GATE BIENNALE

Sisters, Brothers
Stig Larsson
Translation by Frank Gabriel Perry

The Oginski Polonaise
Nikolai Kolyada
Translation by Peter Tegel

Methuen Fast Track Playscripts

First published in Great Britain 1996
by Methuen Drama
an imprint of Reed International Books Ltd
Michelin House, 81 Fulham Road, London SW3 6RB
and Auckland, Melbourne, Singapore and Toronto
in association with the Gate Theatre
11 Pembridge Road, London W11 3HQ

Sisters, Brothers translation copyright © 1996 by
Frank Gabriel Perry
The Oginski Polonaise translation copyright © 1996 by
Peter Tegel
The authors and translators have asserted their moral rights

ISBN 0 413 70780 6

A CIP catalogue record for this book is available from the
British Library

Typeset by Wilmaset Ltd, Birkenhead, Wirral

Printed in Great Britain by Cox & Wyman Ltd, Reading,
Berkshire

GATE BIENNALE

A CELEBRATION OF CONTEMPORARY EUROPEAN THEATRE AT THE GATE THEATRE

Gate Biennale is a unique celebration of contemporary European writing and writers. Based on a European model this is a British first, a biennial festival of the newest, freshest work from our continent. The Gate has spent considerable time researching the most exciting European playwrights and their plays from 1993 to 1995 and the season presents work from the United Kingdom, Austria, Sweden, Russia, Germany and Spain.

The emphasis of the festival is on the writers, all of whom we believe will come to dominate European theatrical culture over the next twenty years. Gate Biennale reveals the energy and wit shared by a generation with all six plays casting a scathing eye over contemporary Europe. The writers are political, scabrous and very funny.

Following on from the opening two plays of **Cat and Mouse (Sheep)** by **Gregory Motton** and **Services** by **Elfriede Jelinek**, we now present **Sisters, Brothers** by **Stig Larsson** and **The Oginski Polonaise** by **Nikolai Kolyada**.

Stig Larsson's writing for the stage, four plays so far, has been performed to critical acclaim from Stockholm to Helsinki and New York. His plays are regarded as the most essential in modern Swedish theatre, he has an unfailing accuracy in the art of catching the language of today, of placing his characters at the centre of time. In **Sisters, Brothers**, the smash hit of Stockholm of 1994, Larsson again shows his instinct for psychological and emotional violence combined with a wonderful sense of humour. Larsson's **Return of the Convict** will be the subject of a reading at the Gate on 10 March at 7 p.m.

In the ten years since Nikolai Kolyada turned his hand from acting to writing he has become one of the most performed playwrights in his country with sixteen of his thirty-seven plays in the repertoires of 150 theatres. His work has been variously described as fine and elucidating, gutsy and full of touching fragility and elegance. In **The Oginski Polonaise** Kolyada plays on Tennessee Williams's **A Streetcar Named Desire** to produce a bleak but human vision of post-perestroika Russia. Another of his plays, **The Catapult**,

(1989) will be read at the Gate on 3 March at 7 p.m.

Gate Biennale will offer London a chance to see some varied and radical work as well as breathing life back into theatrical debate. The festival is designed to ask important questions about Britain's European identity, as well as if there is such a thing as a general European identity, at a time when the issue has never been more sensitive; but it is also a celebration, diverse and chaotic, of the most innovative contemporary work and writers in Europe today.

Acknowledgements

Gate Biennale was funded by:
The International Initiatives Fund of the Arts Council of England
The European Cultural Foundation, which promotes European cultural co-operation by running a grants programme, developing new projects and programmes in priority areas and serving as the centre of a network of fourteen independent institutes and centres for research and study
The Visiting Arts of Great Britain

Gate Biennale was made possible by the generous support of the following organisations and individuals: The Cultural Relations Department of the Foreign and Commonwealth Office, BBC World Service, Jenny Hall, The Jerwood Foundation, London Arts Board, Allied Domecq, and the Arthur Andersen Foundation, the Swedish Embassy and the Goethe Institute. Methuen Drama will publish all the plays in the season.

With thanks to:
David Pike, Bruce McAlpine, Anders Clarsson, Margaret Saville, Laura Hacker, Sue Higginson, Ian Oag and Edwina Simpson.

The Gate

The Gate exists to introduce the work of international playwrights to a British audience. Its acclaimed seasons of work – including Women in World Theatre, The Spanish Golden Age, Six Plays for Europe, Agamemnon's Children and Storm and Stress – have led to a number of awards and widespread acclaim.

Now in its sixteenth year, the Gate has always aspired to produce the best of undiscovered world drama, providing a platform for the emerging talents of actors, designers, directors and translators. The permanent staff earn less than a living wage. All the actors, directors, designers and stage managers work for expenses only. The Gate survives because of their energy, commitment, talent and dedication to work. We constantly work towards achieving public funding. If you enjoy the Gate's work and would like to ensure its survival into the future, then please join our Friend's scheme.

Gate Theatre Awards

1990 LWT Plays on Stage Award for *Damned for Despair*
1990 Time Out Award for Consummate Classics Season
1991 Prudential Award for Theatre
1991 EC Platform Europe Award
1991 Peter Brook/Empty Space Award for the *Ingolstadt* Plays
1991 Time Out Award for the Directors of the *Ingolstadt* Plays
1991 Plays and Players Awards for Best Director and Best Production of *Damned for Despair*
1992 Time Out Award for Best Designer on *Damned for Despair*
1992 Olivier Award for Outstanding Achievement
1992 LWT Plays on Stage Award for *Bohemian Lights*
1993 International Theatre Institute Award for Excellence in International Theatre
1993 Time Out Award for Best Director/Designer of *Elisabeth II*
1994 Peter Brook/Empty Space Award for the Expansion of the Theatre
1994 Time Out Award for Best Designer on *The Great Highway*
1995 Peter Brook/Empty Space Award Special Mention
1996 Guinness Ingenuity Award for Pub Theatre

Karabé Award – Jenny Hall

The Karabé award is a unique one-year Associate Director bursary sponsored by Jenny Hall who is a long-time patron of the Gate, to provide a young, innovative director the opportunity of working closely with the Gate Theatre. The winner directs at least one full-scale production at the Gate and is involved in all aspects of the development and day to day running of the theatre.

1995 Indhu Rubasingham (runner up Pat Kiernan)
1994 David Farr

Board of Directors

Mark Bayley
Kevin Cahill (Chairman)
Rupert Christiansen
Roderick Hall
Jonathan Hull
Lucy Parker
Lucy Stout

Friends of the Gate Scheme

Please take a form available at the box office.

Friends of the Gate £20+

- Your name is automatically added to our mailing list
- Priority ticket booking
- Two tickets for the price of one for the first week of all Gate productions
- Invitation to special events including the Annual Friends Lunch

Honoured Friend £150+

- All the benefits of being a Friend plus
- Listings in every programme for the year of subscription
- Reserved seating

Hero £500+

- All the benefits of being an Honoured Friend plus
- Annual thank you in a national newspaper
- Inclusion on the Heroes Board in the Gate foyer

Giving a donation

Donations of £250.00 and over are eligible for Giftaid; the scheme, operated by the Inland Revenue, enables the charity to increase the donation by a third of its value. Please call the Gate on 0171 229 5387 for more details.

Free Mailing list

To receive regular information about the Gate's unique seasons of international work, join our free mailing list – please fill in the form at the box office.

The Gate Theatre presents the British Premiere of

Sisters, Brothers

by Stig Larsson

translated by Frank Gabriel Perry

cast

Bibi	Emily Best
Paul	Paul Ebsworth
Aina	Amber Edlin
Gert	Ewan Stewart
Inga	Gabrielle Dellal

Director	David Farr
Designer	Charlotte Tindall
Lighting Designer	Richard Johnson
Sound Designer	Alistair Westell
Production Manager	Vian Curtis
Stage Manager	Dominic Bristow
Deputy Stage Manager	Amanda Castille
Assistant Production Manager	Charlotte Hall
Assistant Stage Manager	Abi Coyle

for the Biennale

Artistic Director	David Farr
Producer	Rose Garnett
Project Co-ordinator	Clare Goddard
Manager	Karen Hopkins
Literary Supervisor	Joy Lo Dico
Production Co-ordinator	Melissa Naylor
Press Officer	Rachel Stafford

Sisters, Brothers is generously supported by the Swedish Embassy.

Biographies

Emily Best (Bibi)
Went to Oxford University. Theatre includes Beatrice in **Much Ado About Nothing** (Southwark Playhouse), **The Promise** (BAC), **The Trial** (Oxford Playhouse). Film includes **Nine Circles**. Has directed three operas for W11 Children's Opera.

Dominic Bristow (Stage Manager)
Trained at ARTTS International. Work includes DSM on **South Pacific** (Drill Hall), DSM on **The Isle of the Departed** (Man in The Moon), ASM on **Agamemnon's Children** (Gate). Member, technical crew, Pleasance, Edinburgh Festival, 1994 and 1995.

Amanda Castille (Deputy Stage Manager)
Trained at ARTTS International. Stage Manager: **South Pacific** (Drill Hall), **Fragments of a Dream** (Riverside Studios), **Darktales** (Pleasance, Edinburgh), **The Grace of Mary Traverse** (Southwark Playhouse), **Amphitryon** (Gate), **The Isle of the Departed** (Man in the Moon), **Agamemnon's Children** (Gate) and **Calamity Jane** (BAC); DSM on **The Hanuman** (White Bear) and **When The Cradle Falls** (Pleasance, Edinburgh). Also worked as a technician at the Pleasance, Edinburgh, in 1995.

Abi Coyle (Assistant Stage Manager)
Abi graduated from the BRIT School in July 1995. Since then she has worked on four Steam Industry productions: **Dracula** (BAC and Regent's Park), **Venom** (Drill Hall), **The Hired Man** (Finborough) and **South Pacific** (Drill Hall).

Vian Curtis (Production Manager)
Resident Production Manager at the Gate. Trained at RADA. Theatre includes **Bloodknot** and **Don Juan Comes Back From the War** (Gate), **Heart and Sole** (Gilded Balloon/Newcastle Comedy Festival), **So You Think You're Funny?!** (Gilded Balloon), **The Lottery Ticket** (BAC and Pleasance), carpenter for Hilton Productions and **Miss Julie** (New End Theatre, Hampstead).

Gabrielle Dellal (Inga)
Gaby has been acting since 1985 and has appeared in film and TV. She has worked at the Oval, BAC, Gate and Royal Court. Three years ago she set up Straydog, a production company that promotes new work for theatre and film.

Paul Ebsworth (Paul)
Paul trained at Webber Douglas and prior to this read English at
Cambridge. His credits include Horatio in **Hamlet** (Maverick
Theatre, Birmingham), Faulkland in **The Rivals** (Southwark
Playhouse) and **Women Beware Women** (Arts Theatre,
Cambridge). More recently he has been in Northampton playing
Polixenes in **The Winter's Tale**.

Amber Edlin (Aina)
Trained at the Guildford School of Acting (1994). Roles there
included Angela in **Fen**, Helena in **A Midsummer Night's
Dream** and Marie in **The Workshop**. Theatre includes Ms Henry
in **Woman of the Dungeon** (Tabard), Philotis in **'Tis Pity She's
a Whore** (Wimbledon Studio), Shirley in **The Anniversary**
(Dukes Head) and Freda in **Beside the Sea** (Mill at Sonning).

David Farr (Director)
Artistic Director of the Gate. Theatre includes **Seven Doors**, **The
Great Highway**, **The Boat Plays**, **Guided Tours**, **Silverface**
and **Ballad of Wolves** (all at the Gate), **Hove** (National Theatre)
and **Resolution** (BAC). Currently under commission to write a
play for Watford Palace Theatre. Television includes **Small
Change** and **Chicken Talk** (Channel 4). Opera includes **Powder
her Face** (Almeida) and two Param Vir operas for Almeida Opera
in 1996.

Charlotte Hall (Assistant Production Manager)
Trained at Aberystwyth University. Theatre includes publicity
team member, National Student Theatre Company (Edinburgh
'94), Company Manager, National Student Theatre Company
(Edinburgh '95), Deputy Stage Manager, **Silverface** (Gate) and
Stage Manager, **Dracula** (Steam Industry at BAC).

Richard Johnson (Lighting Designer)
Theatre includes **Fear and Loathing in Las Vegas** (Gate and
Fortune Theatre), **Beyond Therapy** directed by Tom Conti,
Down and Out in London and Paris, **Savage in Limbo**,
Naomi, **His Lordship's Fancy** and **Amphitryon** (Gate), **Loot**
directed by Kenneth Williams (Arts Theatre), Ken Hill's
Phantom of the Opera (Newcastle Playhouse), **Onnagata**
(Lindsay Kemp World Tour), **900 Oneonta** (Lyric
Hammersmith), **Borders of Paradise** (Watford Palace) and **A
Clockwork Orange** (Newcastle Playhouse).

Stig Larsson (Writer)
Made his debut as a writer in 1979 with the novel **Autisterna (The Autistics)** which is considered to mark the beginning of a new era in Swedish literature. He has published three other novels, a collection of short stories and a dozen collections of poetry. He has also written four plays for the stage which have been performed in Sweden and abroad. **VD (The Managing Director)** was staged in New York in 1990, and has since been performed in Helsinki, Copenhagen, Geneva and London. **Straffängens återkomst (The Return of the Convict)** was recently performed at the Traverse in Edinburgh. He has written and directed two films, **Ängel (Angel)** and **Kaninenmannen (The Rabbit Man)**. **Systrar, Bröder (Sisters, Brothers)**, which Stig Larsson both wrote and directed, was premiered at the Royal Dramatic Theatre in Stockholm in November 1994.

Frank Gabriel Perry (Translator)
He is a playwright whose translations of modern Swedish drama include Lagerkvist's **The Tunnel** (National Theatre) and Stig Larsson's **The Return of the Convict** (Traverse, Edinburgh). He has also translated **Grace** (Belgian) and **Hitler's Childhood** (Swedish) for Oxford Stage Company.

Ewan Stewart (Gert)
Theatre includes **A Month in the Country, Don Juan, Murderers, The Garden of England, In the Blue, As I Lay Dying** (NT), **Phoenix** (Bush), **Flying Blind, Road, Live Like Pigs** and **Thyestes** (Royal Court). Television includes **Nervous Energy, A Mug's Game, Rain on the Roof**. Film includes **Rob Roy, The Cook the Thief His Wife and Her Lover, Flight to Berlin, Resurrected, Remembrance** and **Ill Fares the Land**.

Charlotte Tindall (Designer)
Graduated from the Technical Arts and Design Course, Wimbledon School of Art, 1995. She has exhibited work in the 1995 Linbury Prize for Stage Design at the National Theatre. She has a keen interest in film and film animation and intends to carve out a career with many varied avenues.

Alistair Westell (Sound Designer)
Ex-Production Manager at the Gate now concentrating on sound. Past designs include **Shreds and Fancies, Binary Primes, The Girl Who Fell Through a Hole in Her Jumper** (Old Red Lion), **Sunshine** (Etcetera) and **Time and the Room** (Gate).

Sisters, Brothers

Stig Larsson

Translation by Frank Gabriel Perry

Characters

The Julin Sisters:
Aina, 24, *the youngest sister and mother of seven-month-old daughter,*
Erika
Bibi, 35, *the middle sister, a local government politician for the Social*
Democrats
Inga, 38, *the eldest sister, lives on money from her late lover, a man in the*
real estate business

The Men:
Paul Wikland, 37, *Bibi's new boyfriend, sixth-form teacher in*
Swedish and English
Gert Santesson, 44, *Inga's current live-in lover, owns two sweetshops*
in the city

Characters who only appear as voices:
Erika Julin, *seven months old*
Erik 'Zeke' Nilsson, 29, *the father of Aina's child*
Olli, 30, *Zeke's friend, has a Finnish accent*
Lova Albinsson, 86, *the sisters' grandmother*

Characters who are mentioned in *Sisters, Brothers* but take no
part in the play:
Magnus 'Macken' Wikland, 36, Paul's younger brother
Viggo Rehnberg, would be 41, died four years ago, Inga's previous
partner, a shop assistant in a record store
Ted Fries, would be 42, died nine years ago, Inga's former husband, a
musicologist
Carl-Uno Hansson, would be 58, died six years ago, Inga's former
partner, a multimillionaire in the property business
Åke Hansson, 63, Carl-Uno's older brother and like his brother a property
tycoon but on a grander scale
Yannick Quisbert, 26, Aina's friend, a mulatto from Martinique
Öyvind Dunér, 39, Bibi's former husband, a dentist
Sammy Äyräpää, 25, Olli's younger brother, a down and out
Jill Dunér, initially said to be née Kolmodin, but actually née Cederlund,
28, Öyvind's recent bride, a dental nurse
Ulla-Mai Albinsson-Julin, would now be 60, died twenty-two years ago
of breast cancer, the mother of the Julin sisters
Klas Nilsson, would now be 27, died in an accident nineteen years ago, was
Zeke's younger brother

Setting

The sitting-room in Aina Julin's one-bedroom flat, somewhere in a suburb south of Stockholm.

Through a door standing slightly ajar the audience can glimpse a small part of the bedroom.

In the background, the sink unit of a smallish kitchen can be glimpsed. In the background there should also be a hall with a door to a bathroom and a passage leading to the front door.

Worn parquet flooring – at least twenty-five years old – has been laid over the floor of the sitting-room. In the foreground is a suite of furniture: a plush sofa, two odd armchairs and a cheap coffee-table with a teak varnish.

A simple IKEA bookshelf runs along one wall of the sitting room; in addition to a few books and decorative objects, the bookshelf houses a colour TV, a small stereo, a push-button telephone and a black answering machine.

Despite the fact that the room looks as though it has been newly cleaned – a sponge cloth may even have been thrown across the small portable TV while another sponge cloth is lying on the floor next to one of the sofa legs – nothing looks as though it has been placed there deliberately. There is nothing here that feels as though it is on display; nowhere can we discern a fussy or an ordered temperament . . . and this tends to suggest that there is something dingy about it all. But dingy in a pleasant way.

Note

This text went to press before the opening night and may therefore differ from the version as performed.

Act One

The sitting-room stands empty . . . the telephone rings . . . Someone is moving in the bedroom beyond; we can hear a window being opened offstage.

Aina (*from the bedroom, offstage; in a baby-voice*)   Yes you are, oh yes you are.

The answering machine switches on.

Aina's voice (*from the answering machine*)   Aina. And I'm not home. You can leave a message after the beep which you'll hear right NOW!

Zeke's voice (*after the beep; from the answering machine*)   Hi – it's Zeke . . . Come on, pick up for Christ's sake . . . Go on, pick up! I know you're there.

Aina (*from the bedroom, offstage*)   Amazing how much you know all of a sudden.

Zeke's voice (*from the answering machine*)   Yoo-hoo. Aina! Cha-cha-cha. Why won't you answer?

Olli's voice (*from the answering machine; in a Finnish accent*)   For fucking Christ's sake – Go on, ANSWER! (*Fainter; to* **Zeke**.) Maybe she's asleep – Maybe better you shout, maybe?

Aina *comes out of the bedroom, dressed all in white. She glances listlessly at the answering machine.*

Zeke's voice (*from the answering machine; shouting*)   Fucking hell, Aina . . . BA-BA-BA . . . BA-BA-BA-DO-BAH! . . . (*A few seconds later, less loudly.*) Just you listen to me now . . . Oh, for fuck's sake . . .

Aina (*into thin air*)   What a bloody horrible voice you've got!

Zeke's voice   Come on now . . . (*Sound of disconnection: click, dead tone.*)

Aina Never occurred to me before. God, that, you know, he's got such a . . . such a *horrible* voice. (*Moves away towards bedroom.*) Isn't that weird that I've never thought about it before? (**Aina** *stops, still looking off towards the bedroom.*) Erika?

Sound of a child crying from the bedroom; offstage.

Erika . . . you little darling . . . you mustn't, you shouldn't cry so much when I'm talking to you.

Aina *disappears off into the bedroom. The stage is empty again, for a while . . . The child's cries cease . . . The doorbell rings . . .* **Aina** *comes out of the bedroom with a pleased expression on her face . . . she's now wearing a light-blue jacket over her white T-shirt. She goes out into the passage. She opens the door to find* **Bibi** *standing there with* **Paul** *beside her.*

Aina Hi there!

Bibi Hi!

Now that they are in the hallway all three of them are smiling warmly at one another. **Paul** – *sporting a neatly trimmed beard and a new suede jacket – is holding a bouquet of flowers; he extends his unencumbered right hand to* **Aina**.

Paul Hello . . . Paul.

Aina Hello. (*She pulls back her hand.*) My hands are probably wet – *Oh God*, I always think my hands are wet. You'll have to excuse me.

Paul Really, your hands weren't wet at all.

Aina Oh no, I mean – for pulling my hand back like that.

Aina *helps to hang up their lightweight outdoor clothes.* . . . **Bibi** – *wearing a pale grey summer dress – takes a step or two into the flat . . .* **Paul** *remains in the passage; he starts to undo the laces of his shoes.*

Bibi This is a really nice flat, Aina. There's nothing the matter with this place.

Aina But you have *been* here, haven't you? . . . You must have seen my flat. (*To* **Paul**.) No need to take off your shoes.

Although, of course since . . . (**Aina** *realises that* **Paul** *has already taken off one of his shoes.*)

Paul No need to worry, it'll be fine, you'll see.

Aina Of course, seeing as you're *determined* to take them off, well . . . Do go on in.

Once the second shoe has been removed, **Aina** *puts them both in the shoe rack.*

Paul Oh, of course. This is for you.

Paul *picks up the bouquet from the floor and hands it to* **Aina**.

Aina For me!

Bibi Do you want me to help you put them in some water?

Aina *goes out towards the kitchen – simultaneously unwrapping the bouquet; she stops.*

Aina (*looking at the bouquet; then at* **Bibi**) Oh God – they're really lovely . . . that's so kind of you.

Bibi You have got a vase, haven't you?

Aina Of course I have.

Aina *goes into the kitchen; but comes out to them again immediately.*

Aina Bibi?

Bibi Yes?

Aina (*discovers* **Paul** *standing there in this stockinged feet*) Oh, go on, sit down. (*To* **Bibi**.) Do you think I ought to – you know – uhm – trim?

Aina *disappears into the kitchen. Meanwhile* **Paul** *sits on the sofa, he looks round the room with a friendly smile.*

Bibi Trim them. I really don't think there is any need. I'm sure they did that in the shop. (*To* **Paul** *on the sofa.*) It's a very nice flat she's got, isn't it?

Paul Oh yes, it is . . . it's nice out here.

Bibi *sits down in one of the armchairs. She looks at* **Aina** – *who enters with a bouquet of champagne-coloured roses in a glass vase that's just a bit too wide.*

Aina They're-just-too-beautiful . . . aren't these, they're uhm?

Bibi Yes, they're champagne – you mean, the colour – what a pretty jacket you've got on.

Bibi *has a feel of the jacket, while* **Aina** *is smelling the roses on the table.*

Aina This thing? Isn't it sweet? . . . feels just like silk, doesn't it . . . But it isn't a jacket, it's more a blazer . . . I like wearing blue with white jeans. Bibi – by the way, you weren't expecting me to have any food, were you? I did say there wouldn't be anything, didn't I?

Paul No, God, no, we've already eaten.

Aina I've got some crispbread, that kind of thing . . . Oh, and yes . . . there's some cheese?

Paul Oh yes.

Aina Cheese – will that be all right?

Paul That's fine, really . . . I like cheese.

Aina And some grapes.

Bibi Do you want me to help you carry it out?

Aina No, I'm just going to check what there is.

Paul What else have you got?

Aina Don't you think that's enough? (*Smiles when she notices that* **Paul** *has stiffened.*) No, that's all right – I'm only joking.

Paul How would I know.

Aina So you do want me to tell you? You know, if I've got anything else?

Paul Yes, I do.

Aina I bought some wine. Red wine . . . It's Spanish.

Bibi Do you want me to help you bring it out?

Aina But it isn't – what's it called? – country wine, you know what they call Spanish Country Wine . . . Uh-huhn – it's really quite a good wine, I think . . . Well, what do you think – do you think you'll like it?

Paul (*smiles*) Oh yes. I'm sure we will . . . I like wine.

Aina I'll go and get it.

Once **Aina** *has gone into the kitchen,* **Bibi** *gets up. Goes out after her.*

Bibi But, Aina, you must let me help you carry.

Aina (*from the kitchen; offstage*) Everything's been put out ready, so all I've got to do is bring it out to you.

Now that **Paul** *has been left alone, he continues to look around. Nods reflectively to himself.*

Paul (*softly to himself*) Oh yeah!

Bibi *comes out with the cheese tray;* **Aina** *with a corkscrew and two bottles of wine. They put them down on the table . . .* **Aina** *stops – shakes her head, rolls her eyes upwards – as though she'd forgotten something . . . she returns towards the kitchen.* **Paul** *looks carefully at the wine.*

Paul This really is good wine, you know.

Bibi *– who has sat down again on one of the armchairs – looks on as he removes the cork of one of the wine bottles. He has a slight problem getting it to come out . . .* **Aina** *returns with three glasses, stops again – and looks round – very gravely.*

Aina (*to* **Bibi**) Maybe I should have brought out five glasses.

Bibi You can leave that till later.

Aina I suppose, I was only thinking that it wouldn't look nice. When they get here I mean. If there aren't any glasses put out for them.

Bibi It really doesn't, you know . . . no, it doesn't look rude. Go on, sit down.

Aina *sits down – looks at* **Paul** *who is picking out with his finger small bits of cork that have fallen into the bottle.* **Aina** *suddenly looks terrified; stretches out her arm; takes the bottle from* **Paul**.

Aina   Hang on. Was that cork?

She fills a glass. Then she goes out to the bathroom . . . We hear her pour it down the sink, rinse the glass out. She returns, smiling, carrying a clean glass in her hand.

Paul   Surely there can't be any harm in a bit of cork?

Aina *sits down again.* **Paul** *pours wine into the glasses.*

Aina   That's just what can happen. There have been cases, you know, where, (*Points with her finger at her arm.*) the bit got stuck. Here in one of the arteries.

Bibi   But surely that's just a myth?

Aina   Well then, skål, it's nice to have you here.

Paul   Well, thank you.

Bibi   Skål!

Aina   I really think it's nice we can all meet up like this. Your name's Paul, isn't it?

Paul   Yes, it is.

Aina   It is *Pah-ool*, isn't it? You don't pronounce it *Pall* – you know the way they do in English, I mean.

Paul   Well, I say Pah-ool anyway.

Aina   You see, I thought you might have been English, you know, originally.

Paul   Not really, it is a Swedish name as well, you know.

Aina   Yes, I know that. But I thought maybe you might have been English. You could be, after all.

Paul   Well, of course, that's true.

Aina   I mean, you could have been born there. It's obvious – I can hear for myself you know how to speak Swedish. Without an accent, I mean.

Bibi   No, he isn't, he was born here in Stockholm . . . isn't that right?

Paul   Yes, it is . . . I was born in Stockholm. Right here.

Aina   I suppose it was just that it is a more common name in England – than here in Sweden . . . isn't it, Bibi?

Paul   Well, that's true . . . so it is.

Bibi *spreads butter onto one of the crispbreads.* **Aina** *and* **Paul** *sip at their wine . . . so silently that for a few seconds the sound of* **Bibi** *nibbling her crispbread can be heard. Immediately* **Paul** *and* **Aina** *start looking at her – as though the sound were much louder than it is in reality.*

Paul   I'm an *English teacher*, you see. English and Swedish. Swedish is my main subject. Well . . . there you have it. In that sense it was – a bit – odd, wasn't it? That you thought I was English.

Aina   I suppose so. But, Bibi, I've got this idea you told me that. That you had met a – teacher. You did, didn't you?

Paul   The way we actually met was that Bibi is the only member of the council who is committed to not letting our school get split up sort of. Music. Drama. The other schools have got all the good things . . .

Bibi (*takes a grape, looks at it; to* **Aina**)   Yes I did, I told you when we spoke on the phone.

Aina   Of course, that's it. It was you after all!

Paul *nods, smiles at her.*

Aina   Well, you have to take me as you find me.

Paul   Oh yes?

Aina   The thing I usually wonder, you know, if I'm together with a guy. Or say I've met a guy. Then I start wondering what his brothers and sisters are going to look like. If he's got a brother or a sister, I mean.

Bibi   But that's perfectly natural, isn't it? (*Grabs hold of* **Paul**'s *shoulder*.) You've got a brother, haven't you?

Paul *takes her hand – holds it. Smiles, as though he hadn't heard.*

Bibi   Don't you feel a bit warm in that suede blazer? – He's younger, your brother, isn't he?

When **Paul** *looks at the blazer, by reflex, he manages to pull* **Bibi**'*s hand towards him on the sofa. For a short while they stay sitting like that – stretched in rather an uncomfortabe fashion, holding one another's hand.*

Paul   Yes, his name is Magnus. He gets called Mac.

Aina   Mac?

Paul   Yes.

Aina   That's a bloody awful name to get called. If you don't mind my saying so? . . . I mean, you can't help thinking of a raincoat, can you?

Paul   I really don't know. It's not something that ever occurs to me. That's how it is, he's always been called that . . . since he started going to school anyway . . . No idea why . . . That kind of thing can happen, with names.

Aina *cuts a little cheese – looks up at* **Paul** *and* **Bibi**, *who let go of one another's hands and sit back in their proper places.*

Aina   Help yourselves.

Paul *takes a slice of cheese and puts it on a crispbread.*

Paul   This really is good, this wine . . . Isn't it a Rioja?

Aina   Help yourselves to grapes as well . . . I'm so pleased you like the jacket, Bibi. You don't think it's too, too flashy for me?

The doorbell rings.

Thank God for that. (*She gets up and goes over to the door.*) Thought they weren't coming.

Bibi *and* **Paul** *follow* **Aina** *with their eyes.* **Aina** *opens the door.* **Gert** *is standing there.*

Aina   Hello. You must be Gert.

Gert   That's right. Has Inga arrived?

Aina   Well, no. She hasn't arrived yet. Come in.

Gert *comes in: he's wearing a sober, rather handsome suit with a cherry-red tie; his eyes and cheeks bear the traces of the better sorts of alcohol.*

Gert   Do you want me to take my shoes off?

Aina   You needn't bother; it gets just as filthy here anyway . . . I haven't got a Polish maid, you see.

Gert   Oh yes.

Aina   Like *you've got*. You have got one, haven't you?

Gert   Yes, but how do you know?

Aina   Oh, you know, Inga told me.

Gert *walks over to the sofa and shakes both* **Bibi** *and* **Paul** *by the hand — he is totally without expression and perfectly relaxed.*

Gert   My name is Gert.

Paul   Hi, I'm Paul.

Bibi   And I'm Bibi.

Gert *sits in the other armchair, sinks back — now looking thoughtfully downwards.* **Aina** *looks at him, stays frozen like that for a second or two. When she catches herself doing it, she exits into the kitchen.* **Gert** *looks up.*

Gert   Well, I suppose I managed to work that one out — you're the middle sister, aren't you?

Aina *comes back with two glasses. She puts them in front of her on the table and sits down on the sofa next to* **Paul**.

Aina   I got one for Inga as well. So there will be one for her when she comes.

Gert (*to* **Aina**)   She ought to be here by now.

Aina   She's just got a bit delayed, that'll be it . . . Wasn't it you, Bibi, who said that she would be . . . Well, then where did I get that from?

Bibi How was she getting here . . . was she going to get the bus, do you think?

Gert No, she'll have enough money for a taxi, I'm sure. (*To* **Aina**.) She's never been out here before, has she?

Aina Of course she has, God, she's been here many times. Well, many, I mean, I don't know – four times. Four or five times. I would guess . . . What do you think of the wine?

Gert *tastes the wine.*

Gert Christ, what an idiot I am. Of course she's been here . . . (*Looks at the label.*) A Rioja . . .

Aina It's all right, isn't it?

Gert *looks up from the label.*

Gert Of course she's been here . . . I knew that . . . Course I did. For the life of me . . . how can I forget things like that . . . uhn? It's bloody weird.

Paul Yeah, you can get like that.

Gert Do you know Inga?

Paul No . . . not really.

Gert You've never met her?

Paul Well, no . . . I haven't met Inga or, you know . . .

Aina (*interrupts him*) Me either.

Paul Not Aina either. Not before.

Gert (*takes out a packet of red Prince cigarettes*) Is it all right if I smoke in here?

Aina Of course it is . . . Go ahead and smoke . . . I'll just get an ashtray.

She gets up and goes off to the kitchen.

Gert It's just I thought you had children and you know.

Bibi (*she gets up as well*) Oh God, I've forgotten to have a look at her.

Aina – *who by now has reached the kitchen door – turns round.*

Aina   She *is* asleep, you know. She'll only wake up.

Bibi *goes off towards the bedroom all the same.*

Bibi (*softly*)   I'm just going to have a peek.

She disappears into the bedroom. **Paul** *gets up too, goes after her. He meets* **Aina** *coming out of the kitchen with an ashtray.*

Aina   You mustn't wake her up.

Paul   No, really, I'm going to have a look.

Paul *disappears into the bedroom as well.* **Aina** *puts out the ashtray for* **Gert**, *who has just lit a cigarette. She then sits down on the sofa – leaning forward, her hands gripping the plush, smiling.*

Gert   It's really weird meeting you and your sister – at the same time.

Aina (*smiles even more broadly*)   Do you think so?

Gert *nods; takes a sip of wine.* **Aina** *– uncertain now – sits up.*

Aina   Weird in what way, do you mean?

Paul *and* **Bibi** *come out of the bedroom.*

Bibi (*softly*)   I think she's got even bigger, you know, since I was last here.

Aina   She has, she really has.

Bibi *sits on the sofa next to* **Aina**. **Paul** *– who follows her – sits in the armchair – in* **Bibi***'s old place.*

Gert   I was just saying to Aina that I thought it was weird. Or maybe – I don't know – almost a bit – (*Thinks for a bit, everyone is looking at him.*) Well, what the hell should I call it? . . . Almost a bit . . . twisted. That's it, Christ, *yes*. It feels a bit . . . twisted, yes it does. If you'll forgive me saying so. I mean – seeing the two of you, seeing you both . . . Both sisters at once, together at the same time . . . It just feels weird, I can't help it. Maybe now specially, what with Inga not being here.

Aina   Do you find it a bit hard to take?

Gert (*to* **Aina***; after a few deep puffs*)   I wouldn't say that, she's told me about you after all . . . You realise that, don't you?

He looks at all three of them; he suddenly seems very insecure.

And then when I get here, she hasn't arrived yet. Well, that's the way it is, I supose . . .

Paul   I suppose.

Gert (*to* **Paul**)   Don't you think it's a bit weird? I mean, I've got to sit here and – well, you know . . .

Paul   I think it is a great idea. Our all getting together like this, all at once . . . It was your idea, Aina, wasn't it?

Aina *does not answer but forms a 'yes' with her lips* . . . **Paul** *smiles.*

Paul   It just feels right to me, coming here. You know the fact that someone – well, you, in this case – had the idea of inviting us over like this.

Gert (*to* **Paul**, *his voice calm and hard*)   What the hell do you think you're up to?

Paul   Me . . . do you mean – Me, you mean?

Gert   You're trying to have a go at me, aren't you?

Paul *raises his eyebrows* . . . **Gert** *stubs out his half-finished cigarette.*

Paul   No, really, I don't have the faintest idea what you mean.

Bibi   Well, I don't either – as it happens . . . You'd have to admit that you . . . react very, you do react very forcefully, Gert.

Aina   I don't think this is very nice. Not if you're all going to get angry.

Gert   I'm not angry . . . I'm only stating the case . . . You see all I'm doing is making a simple statement of fact.

Paul   Well, look, yes, I mean . . .

All three look at **Gert***; he's toying with his Prince packet; looking down at the coffee table on which it is lying.*

Paul   Look here, to be perfectly frank – I can't see what I've done wrong? Maybe I was a bit too – positive, kind of?

Gert   When I sort of – what would you call it – you know what I mean. When I open up like that. Tell you, quite openly – you know, like this. Who I don't even fucking know. Who I – fuck me – don't know the first fucking thing about. (*Points to* **Paul***, suddenly in a friendly voice.*) I don't know you at all, do I? Am I wrong? Do I know you? (*Stops* **Paul** *with his hand.*) You don't have to say anything. I'm simply – stating a fact. That's how it is, pure and simple.

Paul   I suppose, but I don't really see what that's got to do with anything?

Gert   You really don't get it?

Paul *does not answer. Now he tries to catch* **Bibi***'s eye. She, however, appears not to realise this, but looks at the table instead – lost apparently in her own thoughts.*

Gert   When I admit that I feel a bit – oh, what the hell – embarrassed . . . or troubled – you do realise what I mean by that, don't you? The fact that I feel a bit insecure now that I've found myself in this situation. Makes it pretty bloody unfair of you – it really does – to sat that *you*, that *you* feel this whole thing is perfectly OK . . . even if that were the case – to say that that's what you thought.

Aina   Is it the fact that Inga hasn't arrived . . . Is that it? You know she's bound to be here any moment now.

Gert   Of course I'm not angry with him over there just 'cos she's late. No, it was just – like I said a moment ago – that he – well, he made me feel – pretty stupid. I don't like that, I really don't.

Paul   I really didn't intend to – you know . . .

Gert   Do you know Inga by the way? Have I already asked you that? Oh yes, so I have. And you didn't know her? Right?

Paul   Yeah . . . uh, no . . . I don't know her.

Gert   Did you know about, you know, the fact that three of
her former blokes? I mean – hang on, just listen. What I was
saying . . . (*To* **Bibi** *and* **Aina**.) And correct me if I am
wrong –

Bibi   It wasn't *three* of them.

Gert (*with a very cold look at* **Bibi**)   What are you saying? Of
course it was three of them! (*To* **Paul**, *raps his index finger
against the table*.) But that's not what this is about . . . Not that
. . . Oh fuck, now I've lost my . . . Oh yes, now correct me if I
am wrong . . . OK, the way I heard it is that – and this is
where I could be wrong – but the way I heard it – these three
blokes were the only ones Inga succeeded in maintaining a
relationship with for any length of time. Christ, she was even
married to one of them . . . So the three of them were the only
ones – as far as I know – she'd been together with for any
time. What do I mean, any length of time – a year and a half
or more. All the others were – correct me if I am wrong –
temporary – OK, fairly temporary. Am I right? . . . That's
right, isn't it?

Paul   Listen, Gert – I found that all a bit hard . . . to follow.
You couldn't explain a bit more . . . what it was all about,
could you?

Bibi   What I think you mean, actually, is that three of
Inga's former lovers are dead now. That's what you mean,
isn't it?

Gert   Yeah, all three of them killed themselves.

Bibi   Well, but what about – oh, what was he called? –
Viggo. There were only two of them, not three. He – Viggo,
he was killed in a car accident actually.

Gert   Viggo Rehnberg, thirty-seven years old, when he
died four years ago. Born some time in February 1951. I used
to know the date – let me see . . . (*To* **Bibi**.) Give me a
moment and it'll come to me.

Bibi   Oh yes . . . so what?

Gert   Don't you want to know the date when he – Viggo – was born. The fact is that I know a great deal about him . . . But I suppose you're not really interested? Are you?

Bibi   You know, I really don't see what you are getting at?

Aina   Paul . . . can you pass me the wine. I've got almost none left.

Gert   All I want to do is let him – over there – know . . .

Aina   Paul.

Gert   Right, Paul. I just want – you see, to try and explain to Paul, well, some of the, what should I call them, the basic terms of Inga's and my – well, relations . . . It's not really a relationship, I don't think you could call it that.

Paul *hands the wine to* **Aina** *– who stops him and gets up.*

Aina   There's almost nothing left. Open the other one, will you? That's the one there – I'll go and fetch some more . . .

Paul (*put the bottle down, without pouring*)   You mustn't feel you've got to open any more bottles.

Aina (*on her way to the kitchen*)   It's all right, don't worry, I bought six bottles.

Gert   The thing is . . . (*To* **Paul**.) Just listen here . . .

Paul   Uh-hum.

Gert   OK . . . take this Viggo Rehnberg . . . it was four years ago. A car accident. A single victim. Perfectly obvious . . . it was intentional on his part. Oh yes, you only have to study it a bit more closely and it is . . . But – let's begin at the beginning. Go back twelve or thirteen years. Then Inga herself was only twenty-five, twenty-six. At that time she happened to be studying – just for a term or so – at Stockholm University and she got involved with a guy. Ted Fries, his name was. Read Music, was going to be . . . a doctor – to do his doctorate . . . Apparently he was particularly interested in that, you know that medieval kind of choir music, what's it called, just give me a name . . .

Paul   Gregorian chant.

Gert   Exactly . . . (*Looks at* **Paul** *in astonishment.*) Have you heard this before? Have you?

Paul   What? . . . Oh, I see – you mean, what you were telling me, you mean? . . . No, I haven't . . . I've never heard any of it before.

Aina *enters with three bottles, which she puts on the table with a slightly triumphant smile. It isn't until* **Aina** *has sat down that it occurs to* **Paul** *that he should open the bottle. Having poured the last dregs from the first bottle into his own glass, he proceeds to do so.*

Gert   He used to sing himself, the way I heard it. You know, this Ted guy . . . He was in the Royal Opera Chorus for a couple of years. A – how shall we put it, a young-guy, a talented-guy . . . Well, they . . . they *get married*! Oh yes! Inga and him. Almost exactly four years pass. Then, well . . . he hangs himself. He *hangs* himself.

Aina (*raises her hand rather cautiously*)   Excuse me . . . Listen . . . Gert . . . Could we talk about something else maybe? Just a suggestion, you know.

Gert   All I meant to say sort of was it's such a fucking – (*Nods reflectively.*) horrible way to take your own life. If you're going to do it . . . I mean . . . Hanging yourself . . . it is, isn't it?

Aina *looks at* **Paul**: *which is when he gets the cork out.*

Aina   There you are, this time it was OK, wasn't it – not a bit of cork in it!

Paul   No . . . no . . . this time it was OK.

He gets up from the sofa – pours wine for all four of them.

Aina   Couldn't you do them all now so we don't have to think about it later? (*It takes a second or two before* **Paul** *realises she is talking about the bottles.*)

Paul   You mean, open *all five of them*? . . . I don't think so – why don't we do them one at a time.

Aina   Just one more, just one. So we don't have to think about it later.

Paul *says nothing, takes one of the bottles from the table; starts to yank out the cork.*

Gert   Okey-dokey. Almost a year passes. Now it's, what? – the winter of '84–'85 some time around the end of January. That's when Inga starts up a bloody strange kind of relationship with some guy roughly twenty years her senior – Carl-Uno Hansson. Maybe you've heard of Åke? Åke Hansson?

Paul (*appears to consider*)   No, uhm, can't say as I have.

Gert   Oh really . . . Well, he's his brother . . . I presume you've heard the name? Åke Hansson . . . Really? Well, he's one of the big names, let me tell you . . . I mean really big – right now he's one of the really major property developers here in the city. Well, anyway, this Carl-Uno, he more or less rains money over Inga. That flat she's got, the one where I'm living at present – the one on Engelbrekt Square – well, *that flat* was only one of the things he just *handed* to her. (*Looks at each and every one of the company.*) What? – Don't you get it? A flat! Her flat!

Bibi   I really don't think it's right for you to sit here telling us about all these tragedies . . . I really don't. There's just *no reason* to bring it up . . . Not here!

Gert   I'll be finished soon – (*Smiles at* **Bibi** *with a glint in his eye.*) take it easy . . .

Paul *gets the cork out – with a flourish . . .* **Gert** *appears to be considering something.*

Gert   That's right, the summer of '86 it was . . . and what happens? It was June, around midsummer. He, Carl-Uno, was supposed to travel out all on his own to some place in the archipelago. Hell of a long way out, off towards the Utfredlar islands, I think it was somewhere round there. (*Points questioningly at* **Bibi**.)

Bibi   Yes, that's where it was.

Gert   No telephone, you were totally isolated . . . It may
have taken as much as a week or two before it occurred to
Inga to ring the fire brigade – or whoever the hell the guys
are who deal with things like that – and send them out there,
to the island. By then, well by then he'd been dead *a whole
week* at least . . . Sleeping pills, of some sort, I think . . . And
then there's – the one I mentioned first of all: Viggo
Rehnberg . . . As it happened – this was a guy, who – unlike
the other two – had a number of – what should we call them –
social problems. Dope, for example . . . Things like that –
tablets and shit. Combined with a bit too much booze now
and then . . . Still, he managed to do his job, according to the
people who knew him. (*Falls silent for a couple of seconds; looks at*
Paul.) In a record shop on the South Island. You maybe
know the one I mean . . . it's supposed to be one of the better
second-hand places, that specialises in, you know . . . things
that are a bit out of the ordinary. Folk music from Africa.
That sort of . . . Oh, really? . . . Doesn't ring any bells?

Paul   You don't mean the one that used to be in Vasastan?

Gert *looks at* **Paul** – *who has raised his wine glass.* **Gert** *furrows
his brow.*

Paul   Over on Rörstrands Street.

Gert   Whatever – it doesn't matter. All I wanted was to
give you, you know, a bit of background to my current
situation.

Bibi   Look – what do you really mean? Are you saying? . . .
that . . . that it was *Inga's* fault. 'Cos that's the way you make
it seem, you know, when you put them all together like that.

Gert   No, you don't get it.

Bibi (*looking* **Gert** *in the eye*)   Oh, I see . . . I don't get
anything, is that it?

Gert   No, you don't . . . not a thing . . . As far as this is
concerned, at least.

There is silence for a while. **Paul** *has been drinking a lot of wine in the preceding minute, in great gulps. He looks down at the bottle on the table.*

Aina   Have some more, the whole idea is to drink it all up.

Paul *pours out more wine for himself – and a little for* **Bibi** . . . *while* **Gert** *has hardly touched his glass for the last few minutes.*

Gert (*once more to* **Bibi**)   No, no, you don't get it. (*To* **Paul**.) And I suppose you don't either, do you?

Paul   I am finding it a bit difficult actually.

Gert   Christ, I'm sitting here spelling it out for you, aren't I. Well, OK, maybe that's going over the top: I'm trying at least to give you some kind of partial explanation. That's right. About the way I'm so, however you want to put it, not obsessed, not fascinated, that sounds so bloody prissy, well – hooked, that's the word, I'm hooked.

Bibi   I suppose.

Gert   But you don't understand *why* I'm so hooked on her, do you?

Paul   Oh yes I do, I understand . . . the feeling. You know – in general terms.

Gert (*to* **Paul**, *friendly, almost confidentially*)   Oh no, you don't, you know . . . I'm telling you all this because you might start wondering . . . well, because when you see her . . . then, you might . . . you might start to wonder.

Bibi   Why's that? What should he wonder about . . . Are you saying there's something wrong with her, is that it?

Gert   I don't, what do you mean?

Bibi   That's what it sounds like you're saying . . . And then there's – the fact that those men died, that it was supposed to have to do with some aspect of . . . That's what you said after all. That *that* was one of the most important reasons behind your having some form of relationship with each other.

Gert (*interrupts her, forcefully*)   It isn't a relationship!

Bibi A form of relationship, the one you have with her – and the basis for it supposed to be that two of her former lovers killed themselves?

Gert Three. But let's not quibble about that now. There were three of them.

Bibi Is that really what you mean?

Gert *starts drinking wine . . . He appears to ignore her question entirely.*

Aina The only one of that lot I ever met, was, you know, it was Viggo. And I thought he, Viggo, was . . . *very, very* nice, sort of very gentle in himself. That's what he was, sort of, you know . . . I really liked him *a lot* . . . I saw him twice, one time was at, at, at – (*Snaps her fingers.*) the Central Station! When Inga and he were on their way . . . were on their way someplace? . . . Where was it they were off to? Afterwards, on the snaps, you could see these – absolutely gigantic bridges.

Bibi Maybe that was when they went to Prague and Budapest. Easter – '87, I think it was. Could that be right?

Aina Anyway, then he gave me a hug. Both he and Inga gave me a hug – and said I should look after myself. It was when we were standing on the platform just as the train was about to leave . . . that's why I can remember, I kept feeling just that bit worried that – that they might, well, you know, miss it . . . Just 'cos they were standing there hugging *me* the whole time.

Bibi You don't say.

Brief silence: **Bibi** *sips her wine;* **Paul** *nods happily at* **Aina**.

Gert (*looks at* **Paul** *– as though taking his measure*) You know . . . You're not a particularly passionate person, are you? – from what I can tell.

Paul Me?

Gert I think that's why you find it so difficult to understand me. In any case, that's why, she – Bibi there –

your girlfriend, or whatever you call each other. That's why she doesn't understand.

Paul   What do you mean?

Gert   Well, that Bibi, recently at least, while you've been going together – well, during this period, she . . . you know the most recent time – the last few months, you know what I mean . . . The most recent period of time you've experienced just lately – that period *has a major effect on* you, it really has a major effect on the way you think . . . I mean, that Bibi – these last few months with you – with the best will in the world – there's no way she could be called a passionate person. And you're not one either, are you? . . . I suppose you never have been . . . if we're going to be frank, OK? You've never really been a passionate sort of person, have you? I bet no one has ever called you passionate . . . or have they?

Paul   What the hell are you going on about?

Gert   Come on now, own up . . . That's the reason neither of you understand what *real* . . . I mean really *burning*, really burning passion means?

He starts chuckling to himself; pulls out a Prince cigarette.

Aina   I don't think anyone understands it, you know . . . I mean, not when . . . when it's happening to you.

Gert (*once he has lit his cigarette; takes deep puffs*)   You've got a bit of a head start though, Aina.

Aina (*interrupts him*)   Hang on. Hang on. I haven't finished. There really isn't . . . no one understands what's going on right then, just when it is happening to you. Like, say, you could be in the middle of a *great* love affair. But right then, just as it is happening – No, I don't believe there is anyone who can really understand exactly what an enormous thing it is. Gert, the thing you called?

Gert looks at her in total incomprehension; then takes a gulp of wine.

Aina   You just said it, just now . . . Oh shit, shit, shit I can't remember how you put it exactly. Something about – coals in the grate.

Paul   'Burning', was what it was I think, 'burning' passion.

Aina   That's it, burning . . . That's right . . . But didn't you also say something about a grate as well? Now, where did I get that idea from? Anyway.

Gert   At least you've produced a child, Aina. So you're really one step ahead of us, you might say.

Aina   Am I?

Gert   I was just thinking about that this evening . . . None of the rest of us has any children, not at least as far as I know. No one has any, do they? Anyone? No, I didn't think so. And I mean, in that case you must at least have . . . oh, fucking hell, you'll just have to forgive the language. But at some point – in the last couple of years – you must have had enough cock inside you for the guy to come. Hell, there is that at least. If you put it like that.

Bibi   So what you mean is, I haven't?

Gert   Look at your eyes! (*To* **Aina** *and* **Paul**.) Look. Look at her eyes . . . She is furious, but at the same time, at the same time she's . . . (*To* **Bibi**, *now serious, no trace of a smile*.) At the same time you're what? You're sitting there getting wet while I'm saying this. Yes, you are. 'Cos you know it is true . . . Don't you? It is, isn't it? I'm right, aren't I?

Bibi   You mean all of a sudden I'm supposed to be – wet. Just because *you* said that I never could be?

Gert   I know that you're wet . . . after all, it is something you can check up on, you know. Not, of course, I mean, that I should be the one to do the checking – (*Points at* **Paul**.) I couldn't, because of him, I mean.

Paul   YOU'D BETTER FUCKING STOP! (*Looks hard at* **Gert**.) Look at me. Look at me, I tell you. Did you hear what I said?

Gert *looks at* **Paul***; both are serious – they look at one another.*

Paul   You'd better fucking stop talking that way, have you got that?

Gravely, **Gert** *stares back – shakes his head a little pityingly.*

Paul (*to* **Bibi***; without taking his eyes off* **Gert**)   We should be going, Bibi.

Bibi   How would you feel, Aina? If we went, I mean?

Aina   Do you have to go right this moment?

Bibi   Gert really is being so unpleasant . . . but I suppose you must have – you must've been looking forward to this? I don't know how *you'll* feel if we leave now? . . . Tell me really and truly.

Aina   Can't you wait 'til Inga gets here at least? I don't know what me and him . . . (*Points at* **Gert**.) – Gert! . . . It was Gert, wasn't it? (*Smiles apologetically at* **Gert**.) – Sorry (*To* **Bibi** *once more.*) – what Gert and I would sit here talking about if you go.

Paul (*to* **Gert**)   Why don't *you* leave in that case!

Gert (*friendly, interested*)   Is it a long time since you were angry? I mean, like you are now. *Right this very moment?*

Paul   What?

Gert *stubs out his cigarette.*

Paul   What the hell are you talking about? Uhh?

Gert   I was asking you if it was a long time since you were angry. I'd guess it's been *ages*. What do you say? That's right, isn't it? *This angry*, been ages, hasn't it?

He looks round, looks at the others . . . They all look more or less puzzled. Troubled, mostly. He looks down at his Prince packet; takes out a cigarette – toys with it and then puts it back into the packet while nodding to himself.

Paul   What are you – What the hell – are you *playing* at?

Gert Do you really not understand what I'm saying? What? I just dunno. Oh, fuck it – maybe you're just pretending you don't understand? I get it – that's it. You're just pretending . . . I mean when was the last time you were angry. It must have been a fucking long time ago? . . . wasn't it? (*Starts laughing to himself.*) I'll bet you anything it was! . . . Can't believe it – *you* – *you* – *you* still don't get it, do you?

Paul (*his voice is now somewhat more controlled*)   Get the fuck out of here!

Gert I really think this is turning you on – yeah, *you too* – hearing all this. The fact that – oh, what the fuck's her name? (*To* **Bibi**.) What is your name?

Bibi Bibi.

Gert (*turns to* **Paul** *again*)   That Bibi . . . I see, does it feel good when I say that name: Bibi, Bibi?

Paul Oh, stop it.

Gert Because Bibi is getting just a bit turned on hearing this? About your affair not being particularly passionate. Because I can see it in her – see straight through her – I can see that's the way it is?

Paul (*without aggression; to the point, with an open expression*) You know . . . Gert. Listen to me now . . . You *know*, that you've already gone far too far . . . You've said things here that have wounded all of us, *all of us* here. It's about time you stopped now, isn't it?

Gert *gets up from the armchair, takes a step, several steps, towards* **Paul** *– before the latter rises (almost in a state of shock, like someone who has been overturned by a cresting wave).* **Paul** *suddenly seems COMPLETELY paralysed. He stands perfectly rigid and pale, barely struggling, when* **Gert** *suddenly takes him in a half nelson, twisting his arm behind his back . . .* **Gert** *manages to keep hold of* **Paul** *with one hand. Only now when* **Gert** *tries to turn* **Paul** *– towards* **Aina** *and* **Bibi** *on the sofa, does* **Paul** *seem to struggle seriously . . . Yet slowly and surely* **Paul** *finds himself positioning so that he is turned towards the women on the sofa. From the moment the* *men got up* **Bibi** *and* **Aina** *have been pressing themselves deeper and deeper into the back of the sofa. Both of them are staring.*

(*Meanwhile: the sounds of struggling, groaning and something like barking from the men, only almost-words can be heard, what can be sensed is the feeling that they are trying to get words out.*)

Once **Gert** *has got* **Paul** *still for a bit, he manages to get his hand down to* **Paul**'s *crotch –* **Gert** *lets it lie there for a second or two.*

Gert   Oh my God! YOU CAN FEEL IT. FEEL IT . . .

The doorbell rings.

Only a few seconds later everything in the room has stopped . . . **Gert** *has immediately loosened his grip on* **Paul** *beside whom he now stands – both turn at the same time towards the door.*

Gert   For Christ's sake, I'm sorry. I never wanted it to turn out like this.

Bibi   Are you going to get the door, Aina?

Gert *looks round the room in confusion . . .* **Aina** *gets up from the sofa, and glances – almost angrily – at* **Paul** *and* **Gert**, *as she passes them on her way out into the hall.*

Gert (*to* **Aina**'s *back*)   Christ, please don't say anything. About this business.

Aina   It might not even be Inga, who knows.

Gert *and* **Paul** *remain standing as before. Neither of them seems to know what to do.* **Paul** *looks at* **Bibi** *– who remains unaware of this, instead she is concentrating on drinking a few gulps of wine. She too appears to need to gather herself together.* **Aina** *opens the door.* **Inga** *is standing outside.*

Inga   Hello.

Aina   I'm so pleased you got here . . . Come in.

Inga, *now in the hallway. There's something downcast, heavy-spirited about her; perhaps it is as though she were trying to control her body. Out in the hall she waves – as though to small children – to* **Gert** *and* **Bibi** *in the room.*

Inga   Hi there!

Paul *goes and sits in his armchair.* **Gert** *walks over to* **Inga**.

Gert   You're really late, you know.

Once she has removed her coat and boots, they come in – **Inga** *in a colourful Hawaiian shirt, discrete beige-yellow trousers and red-orange socks to match the colours in her shirt – then* **Gert**, *lastly* **Aina**. **Paul** *gets up, he isn't sure, apparently, whether he should greet* **Inga** *first or offer her the armchair; he moves over to the sofa.*

Inga   Hello. So you're Bibi's guy, are you?

Paul   That's right. I'm Paul. You can sit here if you'd like.

Inga   That's very nice of you . . . What a gentleman!

Inga *sits in* **Paul**'s *place,* **Gert** *in the other armchair.* **Paul** *shifts closer to* **Bibi**; *makes gestures to* **Aina**, *to sit beside them.*

Aina   I've put out a glass for you, Inga . . . Did you notice?

Aina *sits on the floor – so* **Paul** *can now shift back on the sofa. At this point he notices that* **Bibi** *is looking at him with some surprise.*

Paul   Oh, did you want me *to sit there?* A bit closer to you?

When **Paul** *realises that* **Bibi** *has not noticed his question, he pours out some wine.*

Inga   Is this one, my glass? . . . Isn't this the limit! – Crispbread! And different cheeses . . . And *roses.* Were they from you, Bibi? I forgot to buy anything, of course – Gert, I suppose you didn't bring anything either, did you?

Aina (*gets up with a broad smile*)   Stop there, Inga . . . No need for anyone to bring me presents. Is there? SKÅL! It's lovely to have you here.

Inga   Lovely to have you . . . oh-dear-what-am-I-saying? Skål! Skål!

They all raise their glasses . . . **Gert** *does not drink during the toast, simply holding up his glass, then putting it down. Looks down at it thoughtfully . . .* **Aina**, *on the floor once more, licks at her hand to remove the wine she happened to spill during the toast.*

Gert (*without looking up at* **Inga**)   You are late.

Inga Don't let's discuss that now. I do think it is tiresome. I really think it's very tiresome of you to bring that up.

Paul Did you have trouble getting here?

Inga No, not at all. I took a taxi. (*Drinks a little more of the wine.*) There weren't any problems with the traffic . . . Otherwise I would have been – (*Looks at* **Gert**.) What would I have been, otherwise?

Gert *only discovers* **Inga** *is looking at him after a second or two.*

Gert Not sure I know . . . I suppose you would've been even later in that case.

Bibi You know, it really is good to see you, Inga. It has been a while.

Inga *doesn't reply, she drinks more wine; the glass is starting to empty. There are a few seconds silence . . . At exactly the same moment* **Bibi** *and* **Aina** *say:*

Aina (*simultaneously with* **Bibi**) Well, it's . . .

Bibi (*simultaneously with* **Aina**) March, wasn't it?

Paul *puts out his hand, as though he too has something to say.*

Bibi Aina, what were you going to say?

Aina Just that it was nice that you were here . . . that all of you could come . . . I never thought it would happen.

Bibi (*smiles – with real warmth – at* **Inga**) It must have been March when we last saw each other?

Inga Yes, I think that must be right . . . some time in the middle of March.

She is thoughtful, does not respond to the smile; then turns towards **Paul**.

What were you going to say? It looked as though you wanted to say something?

Paul Oh, it wasn't anything.

Inga You seemed so keen. Didn't you . . . raise your arm . . . Or was I seeing things?

Paul   Really, there wasn't anything.

Gert   I suppose I might just as well be the one to say it.
(*Smiles at* **Paul**.) I know – what you were going to say.

Inga *reaches for the wine bottle*.

Aina (*gets up from the floor*)   Wait, let me get it.

Aina *serves* **Inga** *some of the Rioja . . . then pours out small measures
to the others so that all the glass are filled . . .* **Paul** *realises suddenly
what* **Gert** *must have meant*.

Paul   No, Good God, no . . . I really wasn't going to
mention – you know, it . . . Oh no, not at all, no, God. Good
God, no, I wasn't.

Gert   Yes, well, so you say . . . so you say.

Inga (*takes a big gulp of wine*)   That's quite enough of that
now. (*Puts her wine glass down; smiles at the others*.) I could get
just a bit woozy . . . Couldn't I . . . I really could. A bit tipsy
. . . Oh yes. You see I never learn, not me. (*Serious, furrowing
her brow*.) I just never learn that you can't drink like that . . .
That quick! . . . You have to take it 'a little at a time' . . .
What was it you were talking about, Gert? I really haven't
got the faintest idea what you were talking about?

Gert   I was being a bit silly. Just before you arrived.

Inga   You were being silly?

Gert   Yeah – (*Looks around at the others*.) I suppose I felt a bit
. . . a bit insecure when I arrived, you see . . . when I realised
you weren't here and then . . . I felt like I was at a bit of a
disadvantage, sort of.

Inga   What did he do?

Bibi (*uncertain – with* **Inga** *looking at her*)   He . . . oh, you
mean – Gert? . . . I don't know . . . It's water under the
bridge now . . . Isn't it, Paul?

Paul   I have to admit I did feel – I felt really shocked. To
tell you the truth – I did.

Inga (*stares at* **Paul**)   Do you mind if I ask you to be just *a bit* more precise?

Paul   No, it's really not worth mentioning. It's forgotten now.

Inga (*suddenly explodes*)   That's impossible, don't you see that? NOTHING IS FORGOTTEN. There isn't a single thing ever gets forgotten.

Aina   By the way, I've met a new guy.

The telephone rings. **Aina** *freezes.* **Inga** *raises her glass.*

Inga (*looks down into her half-empty wine glass while it rings; tips it back and forth a little*)   Gert hasn't forgotten anything either. Have you, Gert?

The answering machine switches on. **Aina** *hushes the others with a gesture.*

Aina (*at the same time as we hear her voice from the machine*) Christ, wouldn't it be typical if it was him after I said what I just did?

Aina's voice (*from the answering machine*)   Aina. And I'm not home. You can leave a message after the beep which you'll hear right NOW.

Zeke's voice (*after the beep, from the machine*)   Hello . . . this is Zeke. Why the fuck can't you answer? I know you're there. I know that *you are listening to me right now* . . .

Aina   Isn't it typical, it's him – just when I was telling you I'd met someone new – Typical. It's just too bloody much.

Inga (*loudly*)   Gert . . . Are you listening to what I'm saying?

Zeke's voice (*from the answering machine*)   Look, oh, fuck it – I'll ring again later . . . Or just maybe I won't . . . Maybe I won't ring again ever. (*Sound of disconnection: click, dead tone.*)

Gert (*to* **Inga**; *with a dreamy expression*)   I just lost my concentration when – when there was someone here . . . (*Makes a gesture – into the empty air.*)

Inga   What?

Gert   You know ringing here and sort of . . . like that guy did.

Inga   So you don't remember what I said?

Gert   You said something about . . . something about I hadn't either, you know that I hadn't forgotten anything either. Like you were trying in some way to insinuate, *to insinuate* that – you know, that there isn't anyone – (*Points to his chest; lost in his thoughts.*) I mean, not me either –

Bibi (*exclaims in turmoil*)   But what is it?

Gert (*still to himself; now as though enraged*)   NOT me! (*Then looks at everyone in the group in a friendly way.*) Well, that no one . . . that means not me as well . . . Well, no person – if I've understood you correctly, Inga – then no person in the whole world ever forgets anything at all.

Paul (*tries to get in on the act after a few seconds silence*)   It's a good thing that we do forget . . . Most things, most of what we see, anyway. I read that . . . I can't remember the exact figures. But a very high percentage – up to eighty, perhaps . . . of the activity of the brain . . . is used only for that. (*Suddenly notices* **Gert***'s lack of interest; turns to* **Aina**.) Did you say you'd met a new – a new guy?

Aina *just smiles; takes a gulp of wine . . . Only now does* **Gert** *look at* **Paul** *– as though his words had just registered.*

Bibi   Is it all over between you and Zeke then?

Aina   I really don't know, you know, how it will turn out. Anyway – no one *knows* that sort of thing, do they? . . . You can only guess . . . really.

Bibi   But you have met someone else? (*Picks up her glass, looks towards the bedroom.*) I mean – it is a bit complicated, as I'm sure you realise. After all, the two of you have got . . .

Aina   Erika.

Bibi (*put down her glass without drinking anything*)   Yes, Erika.

Aina I think it's a bloody awful name really . . . Erika. It is, isn't it? Don't you think?

Paul There's really nothing wrong with it . . .

Gert (*gets up; looks around*) So where's the loo then?

Aina Uhm, it's out there . . . out there in the hall.

Gert turns around after only a few steps; addresses all of them.

Gert I'm only asking, well, just as a matter of routine, you see. Of course you've got your loo in the hall. I mean – where else would you have it? Where else?

*He remains standing – overexcited, as though bursting with laughter. But when no one reacts, **Bibi** meets **Paul**'s eyes, he turns round and throws up his hands – 'just hopeless, impossible to explain' – and disappears into the hall. He closes the bathroom door – he is forced to play around with the lock.*

Aina (*loudly, out towards the hall*) There's a bit of a problem with the lock!

*By which time he has already managed. A few seconds silence. **Aina** spreads butter on some crispbreads for herself. **Bibi** – who seems to be a bit restless – looks at **Paul** several times – who looks down, the moment he feels her gaze. **Inga** keeps looking at the bunches of grapes in the bowl on the table; she suddenly stretches out her arm towards the grapes.*

Aina (*gets up*) Hang on – I'll get it.

*She serves the grapes. **Inga** then takes a whole bunch – at least half of what is in the bowl.*

Inga (*looks up at **Aina***) I just want to have a look at them really. Is that all right?

Aina (*serves the others, who take a few grapes each*) Of course.

Inga My hands are clean, you know.

Paul Why do you want . . . you know, to look at them?

Aina (*sits down on the floor again*) Is there something in particular. Inga. I mean – don't you like them? Don't you like my grapes?

Inga   Of course, although I can eat them . . . But that isn't it.

Bibi (*to* **Aina**)   What kind of guy have you met? Tell us.

Inga   Really – of course I can eat grapes. (*Looks down at the bunch in her hands.*) What is it? There's nothing wrong with these, is there? (*She gets up, puts the grapes back.*) But I just don't want to. Not right now. All I wanted was to have a little look at them.

She sits down, leans back. **Bibi** *and* **Paul** *look at her.*

Inga (*smiles to herself; talks to herself*)   I'm sure they're perfectly OK, you know. I mean, I'm sure they taste wonderful.

Aina (*to* **Bibi**)   Guy?

Bibi   Yes?

Aina   Oh, I see . . . he's – a hell of a lot nicer than Zeke anyway. Christ, when you think of all the rows we've had. I mean . . . he's a bit of a bastard really.

Inga   There we are . . . so you're in love now, are you?

Aina   Yes, but not with the guy I had the baby with.

Inga   Oh yes, him. The guy with the baby. Could I have met him here perhaps . . . here, in your flat. The daddy, I mean.

Aina   You mean Zeke in that case . . . Erik Nilsson – although he's always called Zeke. Well, I don't know, if you did . . . Could be? Rather tall?

Bibi   So who's the new guy then? What's his name?

From the bathroom the sound of the loo being flushed.

Aina   Yannick.

Bibi   Yannick? Oh, yes . . . Uhm.

Gert *comes out of the bathroom; closes the door behind him. He walks into the room; he is humming – merrily – and rather loudly, one of the more famous bits from* Carmen.

Aina   He's from an island . . . Over there . . . in the West Indies. Martinique. And so he's a mulatto, you see . . . Yeah.

Inga   So he's a mulatto guy, is he? I see . . . uhum.

Gert *hums more softly as he comes in. He falls silent, once he has sat down in the armchair – where he begins to spread cheese on some of the crispbread.*

Gert   What was that about mullato guys?

Bibi   Aina has met a guy from Martinique.

Bibi   So how did you meet him then?

Gert *takes an enormous mouthful: three crispbreads at once.* **Paul** *looks at him – and then looks rather shyly at the others.* **Paul** *suddenly appears to go pale: as though something were worrying him.*

Aina   We've got the same bus-stop, that's where we met. We started talking. We've got a lot in common in a way.

Gert   He's not coming here?

Aina   Here?

Gert   Yes, tonight.

Aina   Oh no, Christ, no, of course not. I mean, not when Zeke could ring up at any moment. He's staying at a friend of ours, Olli . . . But he only lives a couple of stops away. So Zeke could turn up now, I mean, at any moment . . . Oh no, Christ, no. (*Suddenly gets an attack of the giggles.*) Having Yannick over here? . . . Christ! – that would be the bloody end. Ha ha.

Paul (*gets up, looks down at* **Bibi**)   I don't know, feels a bit strange.

Bibi   What is it?

Paul – *suddenly with a resolute expression – takes a few steps away from the sofa.*

Paul   I suppose it feels like this quite often really.

Bibi   What is it, Paul?

Paul (*looks round; but only at objects*) Felling, you know,
totally – totally – I don't know – well – alien, maybe. Maybe
what I feel is like a stranger. I don't know. I just feel – it's
wrong to be like this. Like this, you know. The way I feel
right now standing here like this. Looking at you and talking
about it to you, right this moment. (*Only now does he look
anxiously at the rest of the company.*) Just a moment ago when we
were all sitting – round this – table – and we – were talking to
one another. Because . . . then I was. And just now when
I'm. Going to say something myself . . . it's . . . it's, you see
. . . like . . . I couldn't be bothered. When we're all talking,
you and me. I suppose. It's like. . . . like I was . . . like I was
DEAD . . . That's it. Like being dead.

*He keeps moving his mouth; seems to be mumbling something to himself
. . . Then he looks down at the others on the sofa, somewhat timidly.*

Bibi What is it? . . . What has happened, Paul?

Paul Well . . . there you are, you see . . . yes.

He sits down again; **Inga** *follows him with her eyes – it is apparent
that her curiosity has been engaged. She is about to say something but
looks at the table; instead she takes a huge gulp of wine.* **Aina** *has also
been looking up at* **Paul** *in astonishment – now she lowers her gaze.*

Bibi Then maybe you can understand – Paul, look at me.

Paul *looks at her.*

Bibi Look at me properly – Look at me . . . that's it. (*Nods
– as though confirming something to herself.*) There you are then
. . . In that case maybe you can understand – the way I feel.
Quite often . . . Although maybe specially when we are
going to bed. When we suddenly find ourselves like that –
incredibly close to one another . . . that's when it feels so . . .
(*Thinks, looks outwards; then at* **Paul** *again.*) so paradoxical,
sort of.

Paul What do you mean? Are you saying you feel . . . dead
– when you're lying there next to me? Bibi? Do you . . . do
you really feel that? Is that it?

Bibi Sometimes there's almost no difference.

Paul   What do you mean?

Bibi   Well, what do you mean – by alive?

Paul   I see . . . Are we going to discuss it – here?

Bibi   Just now – you said so yourself – you felt like you were
dead . . . But if I say I feel the way I feel. Like now. You know
what happens? Well, then it's wounding to your masculinity.

Inga   Do you know why she puts it like that, Paul? I know
her, you see.

Bibi *looks at* **Inga** *with what seems to be revulsion.*

Bibi   What? You know me? . . . Did you say that?

Paul   You know, we really can't sort all of this out now, can
we? (*Smiles, raises his glass.*) I think we should . . . just leave
all this be. Let's drink to it.

Inga *seems to be willing while no one else wants to join the toast.* **Bibi**
continues to stare coldly at **Inga** – *who is smiling to herself.* **Aina** *is
now up on her knees, looking at* **Paul** *who puts down his glass.*

Aina   Were you feeling a bit funny, Paul?

Paul *tries to smile when he notices* **Aina**'s *interest.*

Aina   Or was it something else?

Paul   I don't really understand what I was doing myself.
Why I should go into all that. Absolutely meaningless.
Standing here and . . .

Inga   Well. Skål . . . skål to you all.

Aina *picks up her glass;* **Inga** *looks suddenly lovingly at* **Bibi**.

Inga   Skål, Bibi!

Paul   Yes, skål.

Bibi *smiles back at* **Inga**; *everyone raises their glasses.*

Aina   Skål, everybody.

*They drink – sipping – and then put down their glasses. Silence for a
couple of seconds, as though the air had gone out of all their
conversations.*

Inga I really can't pretend to be any kind of – (*Makes a gesture with both arms extended and her fingers splayed.*) greee-aa-tt (*Puts her hands down on the armrest again.*) connoisseur of this sort of thing – you know – the tangles on the threads connecting people. The ones between couples, let's say – as in this – (*Sort of fades away as her eyes fall to the floor.*) in this particular case.

Bibi Ah, but what you said was that you knew me. I don't think I – misheard you . . . and I must say that strikes me as being just a touch too self-assured on your part. It made me feel that you were about to say something disparaging. Were you?

Inga Oh, I see – disparaging . . . so, Bibi, did you think I was going to reveal something sensitive? Which *he* . . . I almost said – Gert . . . Paul then. Which, you, Paul shouldn't hear. Well, that wouldn't be so bloody strange, would it? I am your big sister. I ought to be the one person in the world who's known . . . Bibi, look at me. You mustn't *avoid* meeting my eyes like that. I really ought to be the one, you know. Together with Nanny Lova maybe, I'm the one who has known you the longest . . . if you can put it like that . . .

Bibi Well, maybe, it was silly to bring this up. But, Paul, you know – in a strange way it made me feel so happy.

Paul It made you feel happy?

Bibi Because you . . . well, the thing you said . . . What it made me think – I did. I really did! . . . was that you might be able to understand. That you really could understand – me, you see, even if it is difficult sometimes . . . Well, (*Smiles at the rest of the company.*) maybe this is a bit too private.

Gert Well, no, I really don't think I agree with that, no, not really . . .

Bibi *looks at* **Gert** *quickly – almost nonchalantly.*

Bibi I see . . . that's what you think, is it. (*Then she turns to* **Aina**; *suddenly totally matter-of-fact.*) I suppose you don't – or, maybe you do? Do you see . . . Zeke, still? I was thinking just enough for him to see Erika a bit . . . just for that reason, I mean . . . he does still want to, doesn't he? It is . . . his first child, isn't it?

Aina Yes, she is. But he's so . . . he get's so . . . So irritated . . . At me. Not at Erika, at me . . . He's . . . well, you know . . .

Gert No, listen, I really don't think we should change the subject. I really don't think we should.

Aina Do you mind if I just finish . . . (*To the company.*) Don't you want to hear this?

Paul Oh yes we do.

Aina In his own way he's really very patient, you know . . . With her, I mean. With Erika . . . you'd have to say that. No, it's me really . . . he has a go at . . . *all the time* . . . When Erika was in – what was it about a month ago – whenever, when she was in, what turned out to be, pain (*Touches her ears for a moment.*) here in her ears . . . she used to cry a lot, you see. Didn't she just. All night and all day. She was in pain, you see, the poor mite. But Zeke didn't get – he just didn't . . .

Paul *has stood up, is going to pass* **Inga**. *The telephone rings. At that moment* **Inga** *is also getting up from her chair.* **Paul** *stops – and instead tries to help her, shoves the table a bit.*

Aina He didn't get . . . that irritated, you see. The way he usually is now – at me, I mean. Most of the time, in fact.

Paul No, you go, Inga, you go.

The answering machine switches on – as **Inga** *is on her way out into the hall.*

Aina's voice (*from her answering machine*) Aina. And I'm not home. You can leave a message after the beep which you'll hear right NOW!

Inga (*after the beep; stops, turns around*) What? What did you say?

Paul It really wasn't anything – I was going to go too.

But **Inga** *is listening to her grandmother; pays no attention to what* **Paul** *wants.*

Lova's voice (*from the machine; a very old lady*)   There you are
. . . Maybe you – can hear me, Aina – well, afterwards then.
Later when you – you know, listen – to your – uh, answering
machine. So there we are. Then – you could ring me up
afterwards – at home – me, Granny Lova – at my new
address – yes – Let's see.

*They all look away towards the machine, at the moment the voice of the
sisters' grandmother can be heard.* **Aina** *gets up, is on her way to the
telephone – but seems to hesitate as to whether to take it.* **Inga** *– at this
point almost out in the hall – glances once again at* **Paul** *– who is still
standing, by the coffee-table.*

Paul (*smiles at* **Inga**)   No, no, I was going to go, but you go.

Inga   Were you going to the loo? No, you go first. If that's
how it is.

Lova's voice (*from the answering machine; after a brief silence*)
You see, I was thinking that – just maybe – you hadn't *written
down* – the new number and – as you know – Granny's got – a
bit of a problem – when it comes to figures apart from – the
number three, of course. You have to ring the telephone
company to find it out. Artillery Street number three, that's
where I am living now – that's the way – to ring me, Lova
Albinsson, Artiller – (*Sound of disconnection; click/dead tone.*)

As **Paul** *sits down on the sofa, he sees that* **Inga** *is still standing in the
hallway. As though she were waiting for him to go in front of her.*

Paul   No, no, no – it's fine – you go ahead, Inga.

Inga *turns round and disappears into the hall. We hear the bathroom
door being closed. But she seems to have problems with the lock.* **Paul**
looks at **Aina** *who is now staring at the telephone in consternation.
Since their hostess has failed to notice the problem, he – Paul – gets up
and goes out into the hall . . . We hear the slamming sound of the door
being opened and closed; there is a lot of pulling and pushing and
fiddling with the lock.*

Paul   Wait – let me help you.

He has now reached the bathroom door; he knocks lightly.

Aina (*gravely to* **Bibi** *and* **Gert**)   She's so – incredibly – old
. . . I suppose, she's (*Points down at the answering machine.*) she's
going to die soon maybe. She can't get much older than she
already is.

Inga (*peering out from the bathroom*)   What is it?

Paul   Having a problem with the lock? Maybe I – let's see
what I can do . . .

Aina *takes a step or two towards the hall, clearly it is only now that she
realises the problem there seems to be with the lock on the bathroom door
. . .* **Bibi** *turns to* **Aina** *who is facing away.*

Bibi   She must be eighty-six, Lova, mustn't she? Of course
there are people, you know who are –

Aina (*turns round like lightning; interrupting* **Bibi**)   A hundred
– I knew that too – Of course, I did. Is that it? Did you think I
didn't know that? Did you?

Meanwhile **Paul** *has been trying to fix the bathroom door.*

Bibi   Of course I knew you did. You have to take
everything the wrong way, don't you?

Inga *looks out from the bathroom again; she is now very irritated.*

Inga (*loudly so that everyone can hear her*)   Oh no, really –
Christ, why don't you go first. If it's going to be such a
problem, I mean.

And they all look towards the hall for a second or two.

Paul   I'm only trying to fix it. You might just – yes – you
could simply try closing it. (*Closes the door himself; cautiously.*)
There you are.

Meanwhile: **Aina** *has walked over to the table – slowly, deep in
thought. And slowly she sits down on the floor there . . .* **Paul** *also
walks over to the suite; but doesn't sit down. Instead he stands by the
armchair. Hands on hips,* **Paul** *seems to be trying to fathom what the
conversation is about . . .* **Aina** *looks up at* **Bibi** *on the sofa – with a
grave almost hostile gaze.*

Aina I don't think even someone as smart as you –

Bibi (*interrupts her*) I'm not smart, I'm not!

Aina Oh yes you are – But I don't think – All the same, I don't think you *really* understand how terrible it is – when you get that (*Gesture at the telephone; grim, thoughtful and serious.*) when you get *that* old . . . No, I don't. I really don't, I don't think you do.

Gert *looks down at the half-eaten crispbread which he has been holding in his hands for a long time. He puts it on the table; looks at the others.*

Gert Going back to what I said I was thinking before. You do remember what I said? Well, it was . . . What I was thinking was – it really is a pity, it's a real shame that we got diverted from that topic – You remember what it was, don't you? I don't need to go . . . you know, go over it . . . You know what I mean. Go over –

Bibi The whole thing again?

Gert Exactly.

Bibi Go over what, though?

Gert That subject we were discussing. The one *you* – you and (*Waves his hand towards the bathroom, as though that was where* **Paul** *was.*) he, Paul – (*Suddenly discovers* **Paul** *in front of him.*) Oh, *I am sorry* – there you are . . . I thought you were over there in the hallway . . . Ah ha. You remember it, don't you? . . . Pick it up again, that subject.

Paul What? . . . What was it we were talking about that was so? Ah, that's what you mean – that business – after I got that feeling of strange –

Gert (*interrupts; nods towards the hall and the bathroom*) And I'm sure Inga – agrees with me, too.

Paul I see. Yes – I'm not really sure I get what you – you know.

Gert   What it was, you see, was that you – you and Bibi – that you – in some way. It might sound a bit rude almost what I'm – You see, you – you raised the tone. Do you see?

Paul *can now hear* **Inga** *coming out off the bathroom and his body would seem to be on its way there too when half turned away he responds to* **Gert**.

Paul   No, I don't, I really don't.

Gert   Hang on – Listen.

Paul *stops; and looks at* **Gert** . . . **Inga** *now by the table points down to her wine glass.*

Inga   Do you want to know what I think?

Gert   Just wait. I really *don't* want to spoil this evening by going on and on any more. But, you know – I really did definitely think that you went up a level. When you were going on about that business – you know. You know what it was. The bit about – death. About – feeling as though you were dead. Maybe precisely because . . . you know . . . you've got . . . so *close* . . . And you can get: *extremely, so extremely* close to someone else, you know.

Paul's *attitude starts to change: he looks attentively at* **Gert** . . . *Having poured her wine in small spurts into the others' glasses,* **Inga** *sits down in the armchair. Like* **Paul** *she notices* **Gert**'s *expression, which is almost* aflame *with the intensity of what is going to be revealed.*

Gert (*now totally focused on* **Paul**)   Well, in your case, it's Bibi . . . isn't it? It's Bibi who you're close to. But at the same time – it's just when you feel you are close to one another – you see, that's when it becomes obvious. That you really are *someone else* . . . I mean, you're someone else yourself – you're not the person in question . . . you're . . . you are . . . yourself. An individual. And as a result – as a result so . . . (*Looks for the word; looks up at* **Paul** *intently.*) what do you call it? . . . Alone.

Paul (*looks at* **Gert**; *as though in another world*)   Yes, you feel alone. Can make you feel that. I suppose.

Gert   Unutterably alone. That's it: unutterably alone.

Bibi   But hang on – if I could just get a word in?

Gert (*intensely, bordering on being brusque*)   Yes?

Bibi   All that's just words. Your argument . . . you know, I
don't really understand why you seem to get so . . . you
know, so . . . like that.

Gert   I see . . . what you mean is this . . . what? (*Looks at her
– mostly in surprise.*) You mean this is all nonsense?

Bibi   I just don't understand why you get so . . . I mean,
just look at what you look like?

Gert   What do you mean?

Bibi   You're so worked up . . . And over what? As far as I
can tell, I mean. I might have misunderstood you of course.
But the way it seemed to me, you got all – well, like you are
now, because it suddenly occurred to you that no one – and
that's the way it is, after all. That is how things are, you know
. . . No one – no single person – can – you know what I mean
. . . no one can . . . *lose themselves.*

Gert (*takes up her words*)   No, that's it. That's it exactly. No
one can lose themselves – in another person.

Aina   But what about – in love . . . What do you say? I just
don't know.

Paul *is still standing behind* **Inga**'s *armchair; he is now looking at*
Bibi.

Paul   You see what I've realised – this evening. Well, is that
you – simply – I mean, you simply, don't have – (*His expression
shows him to be lost in thought for a second or two.*) you don't have
the feelings that I – well, that I didn't really – if I'm going to
be perfectly honest – not really, I didn't really – believe in,
maybe did not really believe you had – the feelings – I mean.
(*Looks at* **Bibi** *again.*) Well, that's how it is.

Bibi   I'm such a practical person, you see.

Paul (*doesn't really understand*)   Yes, I see. Of course.

Bibi Maybe that's it. Maybe that's all it is . . . I suppose.
Inga and Aina, you – you know me, don't you. You know
how I always, doesn't matter what the situation is – doesn't
matter what actually happens – it's – it's always me, isn't it?
– I'm always the one who has to – I was going to say 'pick up
the pieces' – who has to – *put everything right in the end*, I mean
. . . That's the way it's always been.

Gert *looks at an increasingly desperate-to-pee* **Paul** – *now leant
against the back of* **Inga**'s *chair. And points inquisitively between him
and* **Bibi**.

Gert But weren't you just now discussing . . . I'm not
really sure I understood – wasn't what you were discussing –
well, your relationship, I suppose? (*Looks* **Paul** *straight in the
eye*.) Or wasn't that it? Maybe I'm being a bit thick? . . . Tell
me?

Paul No, I don't think you're thick.

Gert I suppose all I meant was that there were quite a few
times earlier this evening when I felt you seemed to – well,
that you did think that, exactly that. That I was a bit thick.
You see what she – what Bibi – said just now. I don't get it –
no, I really don't.

Bibi Inga, you understand – don't you?

Inga *has no time to answer before* **Aina** *perks up with an alert
expression.*

Aina Oh yes, I think I understand . . . yes I do.

Bibi But do you understand, Paul? . . . Maybe it is hard
. . . to explain it.

Inga Now, Bibi, listen to me now – You see – What it is –
you just seem to be trying – and don't take this as just another
typical little dig from me – I'm really being serious when I
say this, Bibi – You just seem . . . to be trying to *get out* of this
. . . Oh yes, that's the way it looks . . . You can see it a mile
off. What you call – practical, was it? That you were a
'practical' person? Now, you know perfectly well that that's
to do with your manner – you know, what you give off . . . It

does. Yes, it does. Actually what it makes me think of, is coldness. You know – the way the cold feels as it spreads through your body? And that's what you call 'practical'? Actually it's that 'ladylike' manner of yours – Yeah, yeah – I can see, you're about to protest but it is – that's the reason behind this – this COLDNESS as it now occurs to me to call it.

Bibi Oh dear, Inga . . . it really can't be the case, can it?

When **Inga** *fails to answer; just peers at* **Bibi**:

Bibi That this particular evening – you're feeling the just *tiniest bit jealous* of me – for some reason I really can't imagine.

Inga Now you know, Bibi, that I am almost never unkind. But just take this guy – this guy here – sorry what was your name, again?

Paul Me? – It's Paul – Paul Wikland.

Inga I mean now Paul himself has picked up on this – well, I feel I have to – if only as your friend – bring it up with you as well. Because unless I'm totally misinformed, that's what was mostly behind – although, of course, accumulating over ten years –

Bibi INGA! – what do you think you're – didn't we agree not to talk about that? Didn't we?

Inga I suppose so. But I'm going to continue, you see. (*Smiles innocently.*) Well, I really don't see why I shouldn't say his name – the one I did promise not to mention in your presence. Öyvind Dunér . . . It must be almost exactly ten years ago you got married, mustn't it. The way I see it now, it must have been a key problem even then: the way – well, I've got to say his name again – Öyvind felt – as each year went by – more and more incapable – that's got to be the right word – incapable of feeling –

Paul (*interrupts; his expression certain*) Love . . . of having feelings, of being able to feel.

Inga Sorry, what did you say?

Paul Well – love. Love, for instance? I mean, soon – I won't – be able to feel that kind of thing?

Inga That does sound a bit drastic – but then why not – maybe, you could put it like that . . . *Although* – (*Generous gesture with an open hand at* **Bibi**.) though you're the one . . . who . . . knows best, I suppose?

Paul (*intensely concentrated; alternatively to* **Inga** *and* **Bibi**) That's it exactly – having to live with that all the time – with that knowledge. You know, that – the one you love. And – this is really important – not just love, but the one – the one you live with. That that person, deep down inside, feels indifferent to you – indifferent to who you happen to be – (*Strokes his throat – for a moment.*) to who you are as a person . . . And you see. It just so happens that my feelings – the way I feel – actually – well, based on the fact, that that's the way IT SHOULD BE . . . I can't adore her – (*Looks* **Bibi** *in the eyes.*) I just can't . . . adore you – not if, not if I really . . . somewhere deep down inside don't know for sure. That you – don't, don't, don't – oh no, no – you can't feel that for me.

Bibi *who appeared to be about to contradict him a moment ago, seems now able only to sigh at this performance – and gives* **Paul** *a neutral stare.*

Paul No. Bibi, you really can't – You just can't, can you . . . You're so – so (*Suddenly turns to* **Inga**.) and – you see – that goes for you as well. (*He falls silent for a short while; nods.*) The both of you – you're . . . impervious . . . yes, and that's why I would always be waking up every morning – going over to the front door . . . picking up the newspapers. And then have to go back into the bedroom; go back to the bed. See her – Bibi – wake up . . . and know . . . know that she, Bibi – my Bibi – she . . . She can't look at me. Can't even see what I look like – you know. As I pass them to *her*, put them into her *warm hands*. The papers, I mean.

Bibi We've had a relationship for . . . just over six months. And we've been living together now for . . . well, it will soon be four months. That's right, isn't it? Even if it turned out that our relationship didn't have enough – passion – or *sex*.

That wouldn't make it right, you see. I mean not – for it 'to end' between us. Good God, we'd still be *alive*. We'd still have a lot of perfectly happy evenings before us. After all, life is – so much more. Yes, it is. Life is so much more than – you know – all those things you're supposed to *expect*.

There is silence for a few seconds while **Paul** *appears to be collecting his thoughts – we notice* **Inga** *in the armchair and how with increasing distinctiveness she appears to be pronouncing various words, silently to herself. Her lips move; she seems to be relishing the words. As though one of them were 'impervious' – what Paul said she was* . . .

Paul   But – I see, you . . . Yes, of course.

Once he has said the last words, as though to himself, **Paul** *turns to* **Bibi**, *his eyes are tired, as though from a repressed desperation.*

Why did you say that then, what you said. That I – you know, when I was feeling like I was dead, that it was *then*, and maybe *only then*, that I could understand the way it was for you . . . In that case you would have to – wouldn't you, you would really have to – feel . . . some kind of longing? I mean: a longing.

Bibi   For something else?

Paul   I suppose.

Bibi (*with a smile*)   For something other than you, you mean?

Paul   Yes . . . for something else (*Thrusts out his hand as though he were saying: of course, get rid of me!*) something totally different from me . . . Yes.

Bibi   And you – all you long for, if I've understood you correctly – All you long for is me, and me alone. My self, what kind of mood I'm in – my tastes. What my preferences are in terms of food, breakfasts for example. Like for instance – as you well know – the fact that I'm fond of very, very cripsy bacon. And . . . My body . . . All of it. Every part of my body. Each tiny, tiny little . . . nook and cranny . . . The incredibly intricate and perfectly unique shape and detail of my anus and my naval and both ears. Is that it? What a

pathetic excuse for a human being? What do you think I am
– a golden idol? What are you looking at me like that for?

Inga (*looks up at* **Paul**)   Listen to me now. This can't go on –
you know, it's really . . . uncomfortable. Looking at you
standing there like that – I mean, your need to go and – pass
water . . . is clear as day . . . and still you go on standing
there.

Paul *looks around . . .* **Gert** *has stood up and taken a few grapes; he
is leaning over the table towards* **Bibi***; grasps her upper arm lightly,
clasping it with his hand; smiles and nods.*

Aina   Paul, listen, you really can go now . . . you can go to
the loo now, if you want.

Paul   Well, you see, it's . . . it's a form of suffering, too.
Another – a different kind of suffering. But still even this –
really needing to pee – something that's painful in its way
. . . is a bit like . . . a bit like . . .

*He sits on the floor – will remain there for a while – abandoned –
looking down at the parquet . . .* **Gert** *begins to walk restlessly round
the room.*

A bit like I *want* it to be now. I mean – when it comes to – this
physical body . . . The one here sitting on . . . on the floor
. . . next to the armchair . . . It feels much the same, as this
need to pee for instance, to my body as a whole. It's just . . .
just a question of . . . another kind of pain. Being able to feel
that. Lying there – stretched out on the interior sprung
mattress – almost brand new, bought last week . . . And then
seeing – turning round and seeing – her – reading her . . .
(*Looks up at* **Bibi** *a moment; looks down again.*) what? well, let's
say the foreign pages – and all . . . all those headlines.
Totally engrossed in them – of course. Doesn't notice that
I'm looking at her. That I'm looking and that I know: that I
can never – not with this body of mine – ever be the cause of –
longing – any kind of longing inside her.

Gert *has been looking down at* **Paul** *now and then, as if he were
feeling impatient, almost stressed . . .* **Aina** *has sort of bunny-hopped
her way over the parquet and is now sitting beside* **Paul***. When he has*

finished talking, she reaches out her arm . . . strokes her hand over his forehead. It is as though she were stroking away beads of sweat.

Aina (*with a friendly smile; tries to catch* **Paul***'s eye*)   M-mm – do you know what it feels like?

Quickly, **Paul** *meets her eyes; then looks down once more at the floor.*

Oh yes, you do. You must know. Don't you feel it, too . . . don't you? It just feels – like I ought to. Well, think about it being something that *I* should do. Can you guess it, now – what it is?

Paul *tries once more to look at* **Aina***; can't manage it – shakes his head. At the same time* **Gert** *sits down on the sofa, next to* **Bibi** *who has to shift to one side a bit.* **Inga** *peers with some surprise both at the pair on the floor and the one in the sofa; her gaze suddenly has a trace of something 'aristocratic' – a lazy lifting of the eyebrows.*

Aina   I mean, doesn't it feel as though I should – you know, sing something . . . A lullaby, it must have been a long time . . . since you heard one? Mustn't it? Or am I wrong about that?

Suddenly, **Gert** *strokes his hand over* **Bibi***'s cheek; she startles and pulls away a bit. And then she looks at* **Gert** *– in surprise – for a moment. Then down once again, at* **Aina** *– who is sitting, thinking silently, next to* **Paul** *on the floor.*

Aina   You know what . . . listen, Paul. I can't think of a single one.

She looks upwards, nodding rhythmically; now she seems to be on the point of finding a tune . . . At the same time **Bibi** *turns to* **Gert***; and then they look at one another, in the eyes.*

Gert   Just thinking . . . well, that you – that you looked so . . . sad.

Bibi *fails to answer; then she looks down at* **Paul** *– who at that very moment glances up at her – and at* **Aina** *sitting next to him on the floor.*

Paul (*to* **Aina***; without looking at her*)   You can't think – of one . . . oh yes – one what?

Aina A lullaby . . . Other than 'Baa, Baa, Black Sheep' –
and then I only know – sort of.

*She starts singing with a clear voice; continuing to hum the tune – when
she forgets how the words continue.*

Baa, baa, black sheep . . . Have you any wool . . . Three bags
full . . . Dumm . . . dumm. Dumm . . . we, three tradesmen
from afar – (*Stops singing; tries to get everyone in the room to join in.*)
Is that right? Let me think – that's it – maybe it's 'wise men'
. . . the ones who brought Jesus myrrh . . . Wandering far
. . . That's it.

Gert (*looking very seriously at* **Bibi**)   Tell me? Were you, Bibi,
were you feeling sad?

Aina *takes a breath, is just about to begin to sing – but then suddenly
stops; looks up at* **Bibi** *– who is now smiling at* **Gert**.

Bibi What, me?

Gert Hello – you know what I think . . . Hello – when
everyone's listening. (*Waits until he has gained everyone's
attention.*) I've got a . . . a suggestion – that's it. You could
call it that . . . (*Falls silent for a while; grave.*) a suggestion, I
suppose – The fact is, since I'm (*Gesture with open hand towards a
non-plussed* **Inga**.) well, as Inga knows –

Bibi *now looks at* **Paul***; he looks up at her for an instant.*

Inga What is it I know, Gert?

Gert Listen and you'll find out. (*Gathers himself; tries to
engage everyone during his speech.*) Well, that I am – an
exceptionally sincere person. For instance, it would never
occur to me – to, you know, go behind someone's (*Stops, looks
meditatively into* **Paul***'s eyes.*) uhmm . . . back.

Paul (*with a firm look at* **Gert***; weakly, with a frog in his throat*)
What is it . . . what do you really want?

Gert *smiles merrily at everyone in the room – apart from at* **Paul**
down there.

Gert   It might upset you all a bit. Not you, Inga – if I know
you right, but the rest of you – You see, I thought I'd tell you
. . . about my – fear. About my –

Silence for five or six seconds. **Gert** *looks alternately – twice each – at*
Aina, **Paul** *and* **Bibi**; *with each glance his index finger points down
at the table, and then up to an entirely expressionless* **Inga** *sitting in the
armchair.*

My fear, I mean, of her – of Inga . . . That she – that it will –
sort of . . . come out of. That these kind of rays made of
aggressiveness, sort of . . . oh fuck, you'd have to say it was a
kind of, you know – *aggressiveness* . . . a silent . . .
aggressiveness – will come out of Inga. It's something I've
started feeling recently – these last few weeks in particular.

Bibi   Aggressiveness, you mean – on Inga's part? That does
seem odd, doesn't it?

Inga   (*smiles, then swiftly is just as expressionless as before*)
That's what I think, too.

Gert   The other men. The ones – I told you their names. All
three of them – Ted, Carl-Uno and . . .

Aina   Viggo!

Gert   Viggo . . . I've told you their names, all three of
them. And the way I believe things were. That there was a
logic to it under the surface, a pattern in the lives of human
beings. That it is a road you take. I don't mean it's one you
can walk on. Or that it's a road you can leave and go off into
the fields. No, what I mean is that *you* are the road itself.

Bibi   But what sort of thing is it that – makes a definite
pattern in someone's life? That would mean you could see
yourself the way you said? Like a road?

Gert   It's just that – there seems to be . . . what I would see
as an *unusually strong* . . . self-destructiveness – well, in Inga, I
mean. A . . . self-destructiveness which – in some way can
sort of . . . turn outwards . . . like – like in a (*Suddenly thrusts
out his open hand.*) – flash – (*Thrusts his hand out once more.*) like a
big, one of those huge . . . blue whales goes and swallows a

whole fucking shoal of fish in one go . . . Do you see? Do you
see the similarity?

Inga Gert? (*When he fails to react and avoids eye contact*) Geert!
(*When* **Gert** *– apparently slightly alarmed – looks at* **Inga**, *she
smiles.*) Are you really? Are you really scared? Are you? . . .
Are you really? You're really *afraid* of me? – Oh yes – What a
scaredy-cat you are!

Inga *smiles broadly* . . . **Gert** *looks down, then at the others. From
now on he will attempt to avoid looking at* **Inga**.

Gert It's got to the point, you see – that I'm sort of – I'm
. . . Well, trying . . . to tear myself away from her, from Inga
. . . There's this need I feel – I can't get over it – for the kind
of . . . independence – a woman like . . . well, like Inga – can
offer.

He points at **Inga**, *also tries to look at her – but doesn't manage it,
immediately looks down at the table . . . Then – with warmth – at*
Paul!

And then – then I go and meet . . . and meet you, Paul.

Gert *falls silent, as though he were waiting for* **Paul** *to respond to
this.*

Paul Oh yes?

When **Paul** *answers,* **Gert** *turns immediately to look at* **Bibi**. *Now
he looks enthusiastic.*

Gert (*to* **Bibi**; *a little more quietly, as though only to her*) You
see, Bibi – when I met you both. Well, I . . . I sort of felt . . .
Do you understand what it was I felt?

Bibi *looks* **Gert** *in the eyes, gravely* . . . *She shakes her head* . . . *it is
as though* **Gert** *were weighing something up. Then he looks up –
resolutely.*

Gert No, you don't. I see – it's obvious to all of you . . . I
haven't the faintest fucking idea how to explain . . . I only
want . . . I just wanted to say I was thinking of suggesting –
to you, Bibi . . . Well, that you and I – that we – just the two
of us, that we should go out – for a little . . . just for a . . . little

. . . walk. (*Down at* **Paul**.) What do you say? That's not so bad, is it?

Paul   I just don't understand why?

Gert   Oh, I see, I see . . . I suppose.

Paul (*to* **Bibi**)   What? I don't get it. Are you going to, or what?

Bibi   Are you *asking* me?

Paul   Yes I am.

Bibi   Would it be so dreadful then? . . . If we did?

She gets up; goes and sits down in a crouch beside **Paul** – *who can only look down at the ground. The telephone rings . . . With a friendly and understanding smile, she observes him during the three rings.*

Paul, what is it? . . . Don't you? . . . Aren't you going to answer me? . . . Are you going to be jealous if we go out for a while? . . . I mean . . . is that it?

Inga   Oh, dear, I'm so sorry . . . I think I've forgotten something.

The answering machine comes on.

Aina's voice (*from the answering machine*)   Aina. And I'm not home. You can leave a message after the beep which you'll hear right NOW!

Aina (*at the same time as her own voice is heard on the machine*)   If it's Zeke again, I suppose I'll have to take it.

It is only a now tense **Aina** *who looks off to the answering machine.* **Bibi** *gets up from beside* **Paul**; *looks down at him.*

Bibi   Paul, why can't you answer? Huh? What is it? . . . I see. Well, then . . . Well, you can just sit down there and sulk then.

Olli's voice (*after the beep; from the machine; Finnish accent*) Hi, it's Olli. If you are there, I think you should answer.

Aina gets up from beside **Paul***; but then doesn't budge an inch.* **Bibi** *goes and sits next to* **Gert** *on the sofa. At the same time* **Inga** *gets up from her armchair – walks out to her coat in the hall.*

Olli's voice (*from the machine; Finnish accent; fear and impotence detectable in his voice*) Zeke's – he's . . . I mean, he – Zeke – 's just left. Five or so minutes ago. I suppose – I don't know what happened, Aina. Fucking bloody hell. I looked in – my – you know – fucking – cupboard – in the loo. There should have been loads. Of those sleeping tablets. Rohypnol. And all that weird stuff he used to bring back from the chemist's in the town centre. My kid brother, Sammy. The one, you know, with the death's head tattoo on . . . (*Sound of disconnection: click – dead tone.*)

Inga *comes back with something in her hands.*

Bibi But, Aina – it . . . it does sound as if . . . why don't you pick up?

Aina Why didn't I pick it up – is that what you mean? – Oh, you know . . . these kind of . . . are you supposed to call them 'alarm calls' or . . . just 'calls'?

Bibi Do you think he's just making all that up?

Aina Well, that, that kind of things that's like . . . completely *crazy* – I must've heard . . . I must have heard it – a thousand times . . . . At least.

Inga Bibi, there was just something I happened to come across this week.

Now **Paul** *gets up; looks with an unexpectedly menacing look at* **Bibi***.*

Paul Why are you carrying on like this?

Inga (*to* **Paul***, resolute, correctively*) Look, just calm down a bit, will you? (*To* **Bibi** *with a smile.*) I just happened to see this in the newspaper . . . *quite by chance.* Marriage announcements aren't something I usually read, you know.

She sits down, holds out the cutting she had in her hand to **Bibi***. At the same time* **Bibi** *has got up from the sofa, and so has* **Gert** . . . *At first* **Bibi** *doesn't seem to realise what it is.*

Isn't that him, Öyvind Dunér – and what was her name?

Bibi *glances swiftly down at the cutting; she then releases it and it falls onto the table . . .* **Gert** *tries to read it – but* **Inga** *immediately picks it up again; looks at it more closely.*

Bibi   *Why* do you do this kind of thing, Inga? *Why* do you do this kind of thing to me? . . . Tell me. Why?

Aina *takes hold of* **Paul**'s *suede jacket, and sits down on the floor.*

Aina   Sit down again, Paul. Why are you standing up?

Paul, *as though in another world, hasn't heard – takes a step to the side, with the result that* **Aina** *releases her grip on him.*

Inga   Jill – that was it, wasn't it . . . née Kolmodin . . . Wasn't she a dental nurse and didn't she use to work at his clinic? That's right, isn't it, Bibi? . . . Uhm . . . I think she – I do think she's good-looking, this girl. I suppose that must have been the *reason* Öyvind left you. Don't you think?

Gert *gets up from the sofa, passes* **Paul**, *goes off to the hall; stops and turns towards* **Bibi**.

Gert   Bibi – listen – don't listen to Inga. Let's just go.

Inga   Surely that's a good thing, isn't it? . . . That she's good-looking, I mean? Wouldn't it have been worse if he'd left you for someone who just – how should I put it: had more of an inner life . . . Was more fun . . . more fun to be with, I mean.

Gert   Come on now, Bibi.

Bibi   Paul, I'm going out for a bit . . . I just have to.

Paul   Can't I come along too?

Bibi *fails to respond; walks out into the hall, puts on her sandals . . .* **Gert** *opens the front door.* **Paul** *walks over there: his body like a question.*

Paul   What? How mean not to wait for me. Can't you even do that?

Bibi *puts on her jacket;* **Paul** *struggles to put on his shoes.* **Aina** *walks to the hall; she watches as* **Bibi** *and* **Gert** *walk out. And as*

Paul, *when – a half-minute later – he has got his feet into his unlaced boots, goes after them. Out onto the stairs. When the steps fade,* **Inga**, *leaning back into the armchair, slowly closes her eyes.*

Suddenly all the lights go out.

Act Two

The bedroom of **Aina Julin**'s *semi-modernised two-room flat.*

In this room — where the seven-month-old **Erika** *is sleeping — it is of course quite dark . . . by contrast with the first act which took place in the sitting-room, one could say that the stage space has been turned inside out: what we saw then, we can now only glimpse — and vice versa. Although it is fairly tidy — it's the kind of tidiness that allows a heap of underwear to be lying in front of the bureau. The 120 centimetre-wide bed has been set up against the wall, or so I imagine. The 120 centimetre mattress has been laid next to a somewhat thinner one — 90 centimetre-wide — somewhere in the middle of floor. Both have been made up with clean sheets.* **Erika**'s *cot could be placed next to the window and the radiator beneath it. I think of this cot as being second-hand, from the end of the fifties — with a lot of material and frills.*

It is dark in the bedroom. Light only enters from the sitting-room . . . In total silence for fifteen to thirty seconds. Then **Inga** *comes creeping in. And only now — when she happens to kick* **Aina** *lightly (who has been lying with her head deep inside the duvet) and* **Aina** *comes up with a jump — do we notice* **Aina**'s *presence. And understand that she has gone to bed.*

Inga (*in a whisper*)   Sorry, I didn't mean to.

Aina (*in a low voice*)   Turn the light on.

Solely on the basis of **Inga**'s *silhouette — her posture — as she fumbles to see in the darkness; just from her movements: we start to feel uneasy.*

Inga (*whispered loudly; almost hissed out*)   Where is it?

Aina *crawls up from the duvet; walks on all fours, in light-blue pyjamas; over to the bedside lamp — she lights it;* **Inga** *is standing there — a few metres into the room.*

Aina (*in a loud whisper*)   Hello.

Inga (*in a loud whisper*)   Hi . . . hi there, Aina.

Aina (*in a low voice*)   I couldn't sleep anyway . . . so it . . .

Aina *fails to complete the sentence, as she now scuttles – once more on all fours – over to her duvet . . .*

Inga (*fills in, in a whisper*)   . . . doesn't really matter.

Aina *has crept under the duvet again; but she sits up – with the duvet around her like a vast cloak.*

Aina (*now – and in future, in a normal conversational tone – here, experienced as very loud*)   Why are you whispering?

Inga *sits down at the foot of* **Aina***'s duvet.*

Inga (*whispers, but now in a louder whisper*)   Do you mind if I sit down – here?

Aina   I thought you'd gone.

Inga (*in a loud whisper, almost hissing*)   I haven't the faintest. But, Aina – it just feels – You can say what you like. But it really feels unnatural to talk in a normal conversational tone when you are in here – when Erika is lying here sleeping and everything . . . Aina. Doesn't it feel like that to you?

With a silent glance – and a nod of her head – **Aina** *draws* **Inga***'s attention to the cot . . .* **Inga** *looks over at it; and gets up – then she smiles down at* **Aina***.*

Inga (*in a whisper*)   Can I go and take a peek?

Aina *nods . . .* **Inga** *takes a few steps, very quietly and carefully, over to the cot . . .* **Aina***, too, gets to her feet. She walks over and fetches the bedside lamp; takes it over to the mattresses . . . This makes it a little lighter in that area – not just around her – but also around the cot.*

Aina   We don't need to be all that quiet.

Aina *walks – with a little smile – over to the cot . . .* **Inga** *is standing there watching – very gingerly, not breathing – down at* **Erika***.*

Inga (*softly*)   Won't she wake up then?

Aina   But – why should? – that's doesn't really – doesn't matter, does it?

She looks at **Inga***; but* **Inga** *only smiles down at* **Erika***.*

That really doesn't matter, does it?

Inga *looks questioningly at* **Aina**.

Aina   There can't be any harm in her waking up, can there?

Inga   No, I suppose not.

Aina   And you'd be able to have a look at her if she's awake.

Inga   Aina, she's – really lovely . . . I do think she is. (*Looks down again at* **Erika***; smiling hugely.*) Oh yes, Erika's lovely. She's lovely. Yes, she is. Oh yes, you are, aren't you?

Aina   Not that there's much risk of that.

Inga   What do you mean?

Aina   Well, of her waking up. She sleeps – so deeply . . . You know, I think she sleeps – think she sleeps – *unusually* deeply . . . don't you? (*Looks away from* **Inga***, who hasn't heard her.*) Although – I don't know.

Inga (*turns away towards* **Aina***, almost pondering*)   Though, Aina, it's strange . . . It is, isn't it?

Aina   Yes, I suppose.

Inga   I mean that she – that Erika – sort of has . . . 'Her Whole Life' before her – and she doesn't know a thing about it . . . Imagine yourself in that situation, that really is *strange*.

Aina   Well, yes, of course, that's right – it's not . . . she doesn't know anything about it. Although, you see . . . what I thought you thought was strange was that I . . . that I'd had one, had a child.

Inga *grasps* **Aina***'s upper arm; looks at her sister.*

Inga   Oh yes, that is too.

Aina   Yes it is, isn't it? . . . It is – it is strange.

Inga (*very tenderly, with an almost exaggerated tenderness*)   My little baby sister.

Inga *grasps* **Aina***'s upper arms; still looking at her in the same way, 'tenderly'.*

Aina   Aha.

Inga You are after all, you know.

Aina Yes, I know.

She takes a couple of steps backwards; **Inga** *accompanies her movement.*

Why – why all this what-have-you all of a sudden?

Inga (*when she stops – releases her*) What's that about?

Aina (*suddenly neutral; a little brisk in her tone*) I don't know really – You were going to, to drag me off like – I don't know – Well – You just weren't thinking, not of – of . . . (*Nods at* **Erika**.)

Inga What, about Erika?

When **Inga** *takes hold of her again,* **Aina** *immediately pulls free – takes a few steps back.*

Aina No, come on now, Inga. You've got to think of her. I could – I really could fall, you know. On her, you see. I really could . . . you have got to think about that.

Inga *suddenly looks deeply offended, wounded, she turns around and walks over to the cot – and looks down at* **Erika** *again.*

Inga In that case, I'm sorry. I only meant to . . . Fool around a bit with you . . . You see.

Aina She is still so red . . . I think she is.

Inga From where I'm standing she doesn't look it – I don't think you can see that much from here.

Aina I suppose it is too dark . . . But you know with baby-skin and all . . . You know, if you wanted to . . . you could touch . . .

Inga (*smiling broadly*) Oh no, I couldn't . . . I just couldn't. (*She becomes serious again – after a rosy, slightly embarrassed giggle to herself.*) Perhaps I could tomorrow.

Aina You can sleep here if you like. It's no problem at all. I've got your mattress ready here.

Inga   Oh no, I wasn't planning on, but I thought I'd come
and visit you tomorrow . . . If it, you know, fitted in with
your plans. I've got . . . I'm free as far as. I've got nothing
special planned in advance. Not now in the middle of
summer anyway . . . Earlier this week my thermometer was
up at thirty degrees – and if I were to be out in that – well,
you can just imagine what the effect of a whole day like that
would be. For me. So I thought to stay in mostly at the
moment. Just as well, now, maybe . . . (*Lightning-fast shift
from cheerful to bitter.*) I mean – well, it really can't be a good
thing, can it?

Aina   That means you must have been getting more and
more sensitive to heat, doesn't it? Or maybe – it is, you know
– the sun, specially, you . . .

Inga   It's heat really, that's it . . . the heat . . . I seem to
find more and more difficult to deal with, not that I've
thought about it a lot before – you know . . . You could be
right – there might be something in what you say.

Leant against the window-ledge, **Inga** *nods thoughtfully to herself.
Meanwhile, it seems suddenly to 'occur' to her that* **Erika** *is in the
room; she brightens – and almost immediately she has sunk down beside
the cot, almost crouching.*

Aina   She's just so sweet, isn't she?

Inga   Yes, she is.

Aina *walks over and looks down, alternating between* **Erika** *and*
Inga . . . *As though to really 'take in' her big sister's face as it radiates
love.*

Inga   Just imagine it. She'll be grown-up like us one day
. . . think of all the things she will have done.

Aina   How do you mean? I don't?

Inga   You don't? . . . What's that?

Aina   What do you mean? What do you mean by – done
what things?

Inga *gets up; begins immediately to smile.*

Inga   Well, she'll have travelled, for instance – travelled a bit abroad. Just as an example.

Aina   I see, of course . . . Oh, of course . . . You can just imagine . . . Cannes.

Inga   Cannes? . . . in France?

Aina   Yes, on the French Riviera . . . although I don't know why I thought of that really . . . You know . . . at that . . . At the film festival they have there.

Inga   The film festival in Cannes?

Aina   Yes, she could be just moving around over there . . . among the film stars. (*She brightens and tries to catch* **Inga***'s eye.*) Sure, she could . . . be moving around . . . going to . . . going to one of those – beach parties.

Inga   Oh, I see . . . but actually, you know . . .

Aina   Yes she could . . . Can you see it as well . . . Can you see it right before your eyes?

Inga   Actually, you know what's really strange is that there's a (*Falls silent; looks at the cot – smiles at* **Aina**.) future . . . Strange that there is a future at all.

Aina   That's right . . . and it goes to us too . . . doesn't it? . . . You know that we – you and me, that is, we'll be old as well . . . I mean, when she's that old, well, then, I'll be – I'll be all of . . .

Inga   Forty. Forty-five.

Aina   Why do you have to get in first? You just have to, don't you?

Inga   What's the matter? I don't . . . What are you on about?

Aina   I don't think so . . . I might be . . . I might be . . . younger than that. (*Looks up at the ceiling while she thinks*.) If I'm twenty-four now . . . and she – 's sixteen . . . That would make forty. No, well, she'd have to . . . No, she couldn't – be fifteen, could she? – I mean and go off to Cannes.

Inga *takes a few steps towards* **Aina** – *ending by standing right next to her sister: looking at her with a remarkably steady gaze.*

Inga (*grasps* **Aina**'*s shoulders*)　Now, fifteen – that is a bit young, you know.

Aina　OK, you worked it out . . . more or less correctly after all.

Inga　That you would be forty, forty-five then? . . . Yes, I suppose so.

Aina　Do you know what it feels like with you standing here?

Inga　Not really.

Aina　Well, maybe you remember one summer when you were staying with me, up at Granny and Grandad's – and – well, you remember the room they had that was right next to the part of the woodshed they kept all the coal in . . . that you weren't allowed to touch, or I wasn't anyway. Because it made you black all over, the moment you barely touched it . . . well, just next door, there was this room without any furniture.

Inga (*releases* **Aina***; looks outward – pensive*)　No, I don't. Lord – Do I? – No, I don't think I do, no, I don't remember it at all.

Aina　That's a shame – what a shame you don't remember it . . . Be a lot easier to tell you about it. If we could see the same images.

Inga *looks at* **Aina** *in astonishment 'in an exaggerated manner' as though she had said something stupid.*

Aina　Of course, not the same images, not exactly the same . . . But just a little bit the same perhaps . . . Like when you and I used to spend the night there.

Inga　There's so much of our lives, you know – we've just totally forgotten . . . No, I can't – No – No – it's awful, it's too bloody awful to think about . . . and I'm not going to either.

Aina The thing I suddenly remembered was a – very
peculiar smell from that coal they had lying there – in a great
pile on the other side of that – the way I remember it now it
was terribly thin – there were these ginormous gaps between
the boards . . . That's right . . . Yes, it is . . . the wall
between the rooms was so thin that that smell of the coal –
well . . . was . . . well . . . all rough and prickly . . . it was
almost 'nastily rough'. You see . . . that, you understand –
what I felt – I might have been eight or seven. I might have
been – well, I could have been six, yes, I might have . . .
What it felt like to me then was 'The Smell of Man' – if you
can put it like that, if I could – being a child – have thought –
that way.

*While **Aina** has been narrating this: The further into the tale she gets,
the more enthusiastic and more astonished by it all, she seems. It is
clearly the first time she has mentioned this, she may never have thought
about it before. Several times during the tale, **Inga** has turned away –
as though she didn't want to look **Aina** in the face, and so be able to
remember it better. But maybe too – as if the story has something
wounding in it.*

Inga What got you started on all this?

Aina What? What got me started on this?

Inga Yes, I do remember.

Aina Oh, I see. Well, it was just – why do you say –
(*Appears suddenly to understand.*) Well, you see. I suppose so . . .
that's the way it was . . . Something about . . . there was
something in the air that – you know – it was just something I
happened to . . .

Inga You felt something in the air, you said, like . . . The
words you used were 'rough' or it might have been 'prickly' –
like it feels when you stroke a beard, I suppose you mean. A
smell that gave you the feeling of – what was the word you
used? – maleness?

Aina Well, I just don't understand why *that* should be so
hurtful – (*Looks at **Inga** again; the same rigid face.*) Now, Inga,
come on!

She is on her way out of the room, but stops in the doorway.

In that case I think you'd better go home. Right this moment
– if that's the way it's going to be.

Inga   No, listen, Aina. Aina. That's the way I thought it
was . . . You see – what it was I (*Shakes her head pensively.*) got
– to tell you the truth I suppose . . . In the first place I got,
well, mostly. Incredibly embarrassed. That you. Well,
maybe without your even thinking about it. Sensed, I
suppose. To some extent. Whatever it was. Something all the
same . . . In me – inside me, I mean – in who I am – here
inside my body. Anyway that's where you sensed whatever it
was. It, the thing you said . . .

Aina   There isn't . . . No, Inga . . . there isn't anything
'male' about you!

Inga   I was feeling happy – I just wanted to. And then . . .
you went and misunderstood. That's it.

Aina *sits down again on her mattress. Soon she looks up at* **Inga**.

Aina   Am I supposed to resemble her then? Do you really
think so?

Inga   What did you say? Who are you talking about?

Aina   Well, you said something about it this evening – that
I did . . . Resemble her – don't you remember? Resemble
Ulla-Mai?

Inga   Oh, I see, you mean – resemble Mother.

*She walks over to the window, opens the closed blinds – looks out: there
is a suggestion of the coming dawn; she closes them – turns towards*
Aina.

You can't really remember that much about her can you.
And that means you don't really know anything at all . . . I
suppose . . . I get it.

Aina   You know I've said that myself, loads and loads of
times. That I don't remember her. Not at all. You ought to
know that by now. It's no fun hearing it said again, let me tell
you. Like you did just now.

Inga   You know the thing that is really is strange – is that it isn't only the characteristics you know, to do with appearance that get passed down. Or I suppose I should say: can get passed down.

Aina   I mean when it comes to temperament, that's obvious. I'm a temperamental person after all – and Ulla-Mai was too. But maybe I've also got the same kind of – what do you call it – hot-headedness? . . . Like she had.

Inga *walks over to the mattresses; sits down, fairly close to* **Aina**.

Aina   Did you hear what I asked you? Did you?

Inga   Yes, I did. But it's hard to say . . . You see, Aina, something seems to have *happened* to me . . . I really don't know what it is. It's really odd. But I just don't have – now that I think about it – any kind of image of Mother. I don't have one either. Isn't that . . . ?

Aina   You don't remember anything about her? About Ulla-Mai?

Inga *nods; continues to reflect . . .* **Aina** *walks out towards the sitting-room; stops in the doorway – and looks from there down at her sister – with a warm smile.*

Aina   Inga, do you mind if I replay the tape from the answering machine? So we can listen to Lova again.

Inga   No, of course not – play it back.

Aina *disappears out into the sitting-room – offstage – for a short while; then comes back with the answering machine; she switches it on.*

Aina   I already wound the tape back before, so it's the only one.

Inga   Was that the one I didn't understand – not a thing about it?

Aina *hushes* **Inga** *when the tape starts.*

Lova's voice (*from the answering machine; a very old lady*)   I thought I'd – what I thought was – I wanted to – to explain – this business of my new numbers . . . I've got them here, you see . . . on this tiny, little scrap of paper – those new figures I mean – the ones I got – in the last few days – (*Falls silent for a few seconds.*)

Inga Oh, that's what it is. She's been given a new number. Now I see.

Aina *hushes her again when* **Lova's voice** *can be heard once more . . . And . . . then,* **Aina** *begins to hold her hands over the black answering machine just like you hold your hands over the fire to warm them.*

Lova's voice (*from the answering machine*) There they are! There they are! On the telephone here – below the round thing, the circle – hmm, the circle-shaped – Dial!

Aina Inga. This – this is like *Mummy*, isn't it – the way I'm – sort of *capturing* like this with my hands.

Inga *looks up – at first surprised, then nods smiling.*

Lova's voice (*from the answering machine*) It's a dial, that's what it is. The thing you turn – you know – to get different – one of those – those things – like a nine – or a ten! Ten numbers. And a three and a five and a seven – unless I'm mixing it up with with a four and . . . maybe a nine – and – what? – I suppose – a two? (*Sound of disconnection: click – dead tone.*)

Without saying a word, **Aina** *pulls out the plug; she leaves the room with it.*

Inga (*after* **Aina**, *the first word LOUD – then more softly*) GOD, HOW OLD – she's got . . . Granny.

Aina *re-enters the bedroom. She sits down beside* **Inga** *on one of the mattresses – pulls up the duvet around herself, like a cloak.*

Aina She is old, yes, she is. The way I remember her that's the way she's always been – always – kind of ancient – and later on – from the time I was two, she was the one, after all, who –

Aina *gets up. Still with the duvet like a cloak around her, she walks over to the cot – and looks down at* **Erika**.

Inga   You weren't exactly two, more like two and a half. But you were little then, yes you were . . . Two – two and a half.

Aina   I can remember things – from when I was three or thereabouts.

She lets her duvet fall to the floor – lifts up **Erika***'s from the cot; and then lays it down beside her own.*

The way it was so level . . . Perfectly level and then sort of . . . horribly – almost dangerously windy, round Granny and Grandad's car when I was on holiday with them in their . . . It was their 'old-old' black Mercedes, you know . . . The one they had before the 'old' one. . . . The way it was totally – you know – (*Draws with her hands – like a mysterious form of shadow boxing – horizontal lines in the air.*) totally flat – by the coast along the Kemi moor.

Inga   You can't remember anything about Mother, you can't. I understand, I do.

Aina   The way I see it – that summer up there with Granny and Grandad, well, it must have been the one after the one she – Ulla-Mai, Mummy – died . . . It, was cancer, wasn't it, Inga – there, sort of, from the beginning in . . . her breast – wasn't it?

Inga   I suppose . . . What do you think? – Yes it was, it was breast cancer she died of.

Aina   And it's so yukky . . . I mean that it – that it was there in her breast . . . Could – be infectious, sort of. What am I saying? – No, that-makes-me-sound-like, you know, as if there was something disgusting about having cancer. Poor Mummy – Christ – getting cancer at her age . . . But nowadays can it be? Can it? . . . Be inherited? It can, can't it?

Inga   Inheritable?

Aina   She did have cancer when I was little and . . . breast-feeding.

Inga *walks over to the cot. As soon as* **Aina** *notices, where* **Inga** *is standing and that she can look down at* **Erika**, *she steals away as silent as a ghost.*

Inga (*without looking up*)   What is it? Are you going? What's the matter?

Aina *stops at the doorway; she turns towards* **Inga** *who is now looking at her with an inquisitive gaze, almost a smile.*

Inga (*whispering again; hisses forth a loud whisper*)   What is it? Are you off somewhere? . . . Tell me. What's the matter with you?

Aina *walks back a few paces into the room.*

Inga (*now and in future in a normal voice*)   It just looked as if . . .

She falls silent, looks down at **Erika** *again – lying there without a blanket.*

Aina (*suddenly seems very uncertain*)   Yes – what is it?

Inga (*looking at* **Aina** *with a steady gaze*)   It looked as if you were – well, *afraid of me* kind of. (*Down at* **Erika** *once more.*) And why – why – haven't you got any . . . clothes on her?

Aina   Only because she doesn't seem to . . . like having them on, that's the way it seems. (*She walks over to* **Inga** *beside the cot; nods down at* **Erika**.) Maybe she feels she's getting a bit too sweaty. And that that – being like that is sort of yukky . . . Dunno.

Inga *looks down the whole time – at the silently sleeping* **Erika**.

Inga   You can't make it out – not clearly.

Aina   I suppose, make out what clearly? That she's a girl, is that it?

Inga (*looks up – and down; after a few seconds*)   Yes, that she has got something of . . . You idiot! You know perfectly well I mean . . . You know . . . family characteristics, or whatever you're supposed to call it? – You know – that she's got some of –

Inga *looks up from the cot, smiles at* **Aina***; points to* **Aina***.*

Aina Something of me? Or – of us, do you mean? Something of the both of us?

Inga Well, it's not the kind of thing you can see from the outside like this. Not like this, no. Not from the outside.

Aina *sits down by the radiator below the window; she looks up at* **Inga***, who picks up* **Erika***'s blanket – and redoes her bedclothes.*

Aina Inga.

Inga Yes.

Aina Inga.

Inga You know – it feels nice – looking after a child, like this . . . What is it?

Aina Has anyone ever told you?

Inga What?

Aina That you've got – a really . . . lovely smile . . . you know.

Inga Thanks. What a lovely compliment . . . Thank you.

It is only when **Inga** *goes and sits down beside* **Aina** *that she smiles again.*

Aina Was it really true, what you said . . . Did you mean it? What you said . . . a while ago?

Inga What was that?

Aina About me being afraid of you . . . ? Did you?

Inga Oh, I see. Yes. yes.

Aina It did sound sort of . . . scary . . . in a way, you know.

Inga I really don't know . . . But . . . the thing was, it looked as though you were about to . . . I don't know: sneak out of the room, maybe. That was it.

Aina I see. Did it really? Well, that is strange, isn't it?

Inga It did look peculiar . . . you know, when you were standing there and . . .

Aina When I was standing in the doorway? . . . You mean then?

Inga Yes, it was as if . . . when you were standing there . . . it was as if . . . (*Falls silent for a second or two.*) It was as if, when you – realised that I – that I had seen that . . . well, that Erika didn't have any clothes on – at all. It was as if you suddenly seemed – and I'm only telling you the impression I got, I could be wrong after all – But you seemed: afraid – or, maybe, embarrassed, in some way. Just for a second or two.

Aina Embarrassed? . . . Why should I – you know – be that? Tell me.

Inga That's the way it looked, that's all . . . Sometimes things look as if – somehow – things weren't right. And then you get ideas about why they are that way – they could be, you know, they-could-be-wrong, they-could-be-wrong – You could just be imagining things after all.

Aina Did it look – like I was about to go out? – to leave?

Inga *looks at* **Aina** – *very gravely* – *but says nothing*.

Aina You know, I don't think I was really thinking about anything at all just then . . . when I went over there – to the door.

Inga Oh yes.

Aina No, that's the way it was, I'm sure.

Inga Well, I suppose – after all, you can always – you know, be imagining – well, loads of things.

Aina Yes, I suppose.

Inga Don't you do that?

Aina Imagine things?

Inga Yes.

Aina Oh yes, yes, of course – God. I imagine quite a few things.

Aina *nods to herself – it seems she has started to brighten up due to something she has just thought of.*

Aina But it – that's only sort of – if you get my? . . . inside myself . . . They're only mine then, no one else's.

Inga I've always been very fond of my own imaginings. They are just as much mine and mine alone – well, as yours are for you . . . You see – it's like the phlegm you get, you know, when you've got – a bit of a cold. Like the one I've got just now.

Aina *looks at* **Inga**. *And* **Inga** *can see that she doesn't understand.*

Inga Yes, you know – the kind of phlegm you get in your throat.

Aina Yes . . . I know what that is.

Inga I mean, as a comparison with – your own imaginings. That kind of phlegm – at the back of your throat.

Aina Uh-hum.

Inga That sort of yellow phlegm – the kind it doesn't really do any real harm if you just swallow or – well, have a taste of it there, at the back . . . of your throat – Not, not, I mean (*Smiles broadly at* **Aina**.) that, I suppose you wouldn't just accept, of your own free will I mean, a little of my phlegm . . . I could spit it, you see, down – into your mouth – if you – if you – if you opened it . . . Open it just a tiny bit more and you'll see.

Aina *stares at* **Inga** – *who smiles (suddenly very, very happy) and makes a gesture out over the floor.*

Inga If you could just lie down first.

Inga *laughs at* **Aina**'s *reaction* – *when* **Aina** *pulls away a touch.*

Aina Jesus Christ – you know, at first I didn't realise you were . . . God, Inga . . . at first I didn't realise you were – pulling my leg.

Inga Now maybe you understand what I meant – by that . . . by the fact that you – that your – what did we call them – uhm uhm – Imaginings, that's it. The fact that the things we imagine, that we walk around with, they can't – really be shared with anyone else.

Aina *nods;* **Inga** *looks at her – but then continues to look straight out into the room.*

Inga   Just imagine what Bibi is lying there thinking about now – about that photo, I mean.

Aina   Which one?

Inga   You remember I went to fetch a cutting from the newspaper . . . the one I showed to Bibi. Just – before they left?

Aina   Oh yes. The one you found in the paper last week.

Inga   He did look just like him, didn't he?

Aina   The man in the photo? You mean Öyvind?

Inga   That's right, he looked just like him, didn't he?

Aina   You don't mean it wasn't – wasn't that him, then?

Inga   No, I just happened to see it when I was opening the paper – I think it was last Monday – the picture of that guy. Right there among the marriage announcements and all. What about that? . . . Say what you like, he was very like him – Wasn't he?

Aina   So it wasn't Öyvind then and his – his new wife?

Inga   All I know is that he was supposed to have got remarried recently. To a younger woman, to some *dental nurse* who worked for him . . . and who – if I remember rightly – was called that. Jill, I mean – her Christian name . . . And since she – Bibi – reacted as she did it must have been true, mustn't it?

Aina   So you just made it up then? That her name was – the woman in the photo – that that was her name? What did you say it was? Jill?

Inga   And now Bibi will go around – maybe for the next five or six years or so – well, for as long as you like really – with that totally innocent woman in her mind – as a – I'm not sure what to call it? – an image of pure . . . Every time she hates anyone in the future, she'll see . . . THAT PICTURE!

Inga *suddenly lies down on the floor; stretches out with a smile.*

Aina   Now I get it. You . . . did it – well, because of them, because they – you know. (*Falls silent, nods to herself.*) Yes, I see.

Inga   What?

Aina   Well, they, you know, him, Gert and – Bibi. The fact that. Well, he sort of, you know, started to . . . well – *didn't he*? That's what it looked like . . . Like he was trying to get off with her. That's what it looked like, anyway – to me.

Aina *glances down at* **Inga** *with a very dark look.*

Aina   Inga, listen.

Inga *looks questioningly – but still smiling – up at* **Aina**.

Aina   (*brightens up as though relieved; after a while*)   You know . . . You – you're still smiling anyway. So it didn't make you angry then?

Inga   I didn't hear – I . . . really didn't hear what you said?

Aina   Well, it doesn't matter then.

Inga   You see – I . . . I just happened to remember – that I did – well, I did say that she was called, that her surname was Kolmodin, didn't I? You know that . . . Jill?

Aina   I just don't remember. Did you? When you? – I just don't know.

Inga   Yes, I did . . . And she can't, she can't have been . . . Oh no. (*Shakes her head to herself.*) She couldn't have been . . . Cederlund – that's what I think she was really called – yes, that was it . . . So it could all fall apart because of that . . . If it occurs to Bibi – that it was the wrong name.

Aina   What did you say she was called?

Inga   Kolmodin. Jill Kolmodin, that's what I think I said . . . I must have got that . . . (*Still lying down; lifts up her hands.*) Oh yes, you know what – I must have – got it from one of the names of the writers of a lot of the hymns in the

hymnbook. There was one in particular – that I remember I
liked singing a lot when we used to sing in the school choir!

Aina (*suddenly as though she was bursting with laughter*)   I really
don't think she will have thought of that. To be – per . . .
fectly – frank. Oh no no, not on your life.

Inga *suddenly sits up; flips over into appearing immensely serious –
and soon increasingly absent . . . after a few seconds* **Aina** *stretches
forward and looks up at her; she immediately notices the change.*

Aina   Inga! (*When she fails to get any reaction.*) Inga-a-a,
what's the matter?

Inga   It was just that . . . (*Turns to* **Aina**.) It was just that –
what I was talking about just then – you know the school
choir – And then – and then – without intending to I started
to think about Ted. My first husband – I mean, you know
. . . Because he . . . he used to sing.

Aina (*at the same time as* **Inga**)   In a choir.

Inga *looks in surprise at her.* **Aina** *looks a bit embarrassed.*

Aina   Yes.

Inga   Yes?

Aina   It just felt like you were going to say that.

Inga   Yes. Well . . . he . . . you see . . . I was thinking about
. . . I suddenly happened to, like just before . . . The way he –
you know, Ted, I mean . . . The way his voice sounded . . . It
came to me. (*Nods to herself, completely involved with her memory
now.*) Exactly . . . exactly the way his voice sounded – when
he was singing a – that's it – it was a solo he used to sing . . . in
– in one of the churches in Stockholm. I can't remember
which of them it was, and, you know, I don't remember what
it was he was singing. Though –

She falls silent – and then she lies down on the floor again . . . **Aina**
looks down at her; as though considering the problem, nodding slightly.

Aina   All you remember is the way his voice sounded. I see.

Inga   You know, Aina . . . (*Falls silent.*)

Aina (*peers down – brings her face close to* **Inga**'s)   What?

When **Inga** *now opens her eyes,* **Aina** *pulls back – sits herself down . . . leaning against the radiator.*

Inga   You see, when Gert this evening was . . . You remember, don't you? You remember, he – (*She suddenly sits up; looks – now soberly – at* **Aina**.) I'm sure you remember the way he, Gert, kept droning on about – well, that I sort of – I don't really know for sure what he meant. Well, anyway that – that in some way . . . I, you know, frightened him, I don't know . . . He . . . He'd, as far as I could make out – he did say – he did say something about it, he did, didn't he? You know – something about them . . . I mean: Ted and . . . Carl-Uno Hansson, you know. And – Viggo –

Aina (*at the same time as* **Inga**)   Viggo.

Inga *now looks questioningly – almost challengingly – at* **Aina** . . . *And* **Aina** *– her eyes immediately start to wander. She says nothing.*

Inga   Well, he did talk about them, I suppose . . . Didn't he? I don't see why that should make you look so embarrassed?

Aina   No, I'm not . . . You see, he – Gert – he – he did say something about that. That they – well, that they had died then and so on. Viggo in, well, a car accident it was, wasn't it?

Inga   He must have said that they were all dead, all three of them. And bound to have, that Viggo – although it hasn't been officially certified yet as it – well – yes – it was his own will, after all, that it should turn out the way it did – though. (*Huddles in on herself, as though she were cold.*) Though – will? (*After a hasty smile at* **Aina**.) His own will – that's overdoing it a bit, maybe. Maybe really . . . maybe you'd – yes, you'd have to say it was – wrong, it's wrong isn't it, Aina – calling something like that – his own will – don't you think?

Aina   I see, how do you, what do you mean? . . . his will – to take his own life?

Inga (*suddenly looks in surprise at* **Aina**) What? What are you on about?

Aina *looks uncertain – and rapidly – unhappy.*

Aina Yes.

Quite suddenly – without any kind of warning – **Inga** *starts to cry;* **Aina**, *immediately scared stiff, tries in some way – if not to embrace her sister – at least to touch her. Touch one of her shoulders; with an anxiously benevolent expression of wanting to bring comfort. But . . . now it is as if – grief – or the perfect darkness of a cave – is trying to crawl out of* **Inga**'s *body.*

Aina Inga . . . Inga.

Gradually **Inga** *calms down. She seems to bring herself back down into the room. And finally: she is capable of looking at* **Aina**, *to meet her baby sister's enquiring gaze.*

Inga Do you think I wanted it to turn out like this?

Aina No, I don't. I really don't think that.

Inga It's really not . . . it's not my fault, it's not, Aina – that they all sort of . . . end up . . . so insecure.

Aina Of course, it isn't. It couldn't be.

Inga The way – the way just now Bibi was . . . trying maybe – in that rather, you know, clumsy way of hers . . . to imitate . . . just now . . . in a way, I mean, Don't you think?

She looks at **Aina** *– and simultaneously dries her teared face with the Hawaiian shirt.* **Aina** *nods gravely, says nothing.*

(*Suddenly whispering again, a loud whisper.*) You do understand what I mean?

Aina Yes, I do.

Inga *lies down on the floor again; and* **Aina** *looks at her but seems not to know what to do – then she lies down too, next to her big sister* **Inga**.

Aina (*once on the floor, up to the ceiling*) Yes, I do . . . I do understand.

Inga *suddenly sits up; looks with immense tenderness – down at her sister.*

Inga   You really do understand so much more than any one could believe. Yes, you do, you know.

Aina (*still lying down, disturbed*)   Do I? . . . What do I? . . . What do you mean, then, what sort of thing?

Inga   You're still the little child, Aina.

And then: this, too, without the slightest warning – Inga begins to nuzzle or grub with her head against her (**Aina**'s *) stomach and chest . . .* **Aina** *screams now and then – her whole body jerks crazily as she tries to escape – as though she were being tickled or . . . being frightened.*

Inga (*extremely affected, like the ghost in a children's programme for three- to five-year-olds*)   IIIII HAAAAVE TOOOO HAAAAVE THHIIIIS NEEWW . . . HAAVVE TTOO HAAVE THIIIIS YUMMMMYYY TUMMMY MUMMMY . . . IIII . . . MUUSST HAAAAVE THIIIIS YUMMMYY NOOOW, OOOHH YEESS III DOOO!

The telephone rings – out in the sitting-room.

(*Equally affected, but now with another voice – more like in a game for three-year-olds.*) Yummy-yummy. Can I have them now. Yummy-mummy. I want it now.

Aina's voice (*from the answering machine*)   Aina. And I'm not home. You can leave a message after the beep which you'll hear right NOW!

But when we hear that it is **Zeke's voice** *– both* **Inga** *and* **Aina** *stand up at precisely the same instant 'with the precision of circus artists'. Soon* **Aina** *has crept silently out of the room, offstage . . .* **Inga** *walks over to the doorway; sits there on the threshold.*

Zeke's voice (*from the answering machine*)   Aina . . . Aina. I betcha dunno where I am then? And listen, d'you know what else? I betcha dunno – I've got someone with me. Oh yes I have. Aina – you'll never guess, no, you won't, who I've got here.

Aina (*from the sitting-room; offstage; shouting loudly*)   It's Olli's baby brother. It's that idiot Sammy, you've got with you – anyway what the fuck do I care?

Zeke's voice (*from the answering machine*)   Listen, you . . . You've never seen this man, not this one – because, you see, he – the one I've got with me. On the way in now, you know. Bloody far in. (*Suddenly a groaning sound from* **Zeke** *on the answering machine.*)

Inga – *sitting there on the threshold, turned away, looking out into the room* – *moves her head in time with* **Zeke***'s groans* – *during the five to ten seconds the sound continues.*

Zeke's voice (*from the answering machine*)   HE's – no other than – fuck it, y'know – my little brother Klas. You know, the one I told you about, the one, you know, who got hold of some fucking high tension cable and was sort of – well, kind of got grilled, I suppose. When I was ten, and he'd just turned eight – (*Sound of disconnection: click/dead tone.*)

Aina's voice (*from the sitting-room; almost shrieking – offstage*)   GOD, THE WAY YOU GO ON . . . You're sick to the bottom of your fucking soul; off your fucking head . . . all the way down to the shit.

Inga   I mean. Christ. Was that him? He may be . . . you know. He could be . . . (*Gets up; looks.*) Aina? . . . What's?

The telephone rings again – during the three rings it is absolutely silent in **Aina***'s two-room flat. The answering machine switches on.*

Aina's voice (*from the answering machine*)   Aina. And I'm not home. You can leave a message after the beep which you'll hear right NOW!

Zeke's voice (*from the answering machine*)   You gonna listen now, Aina Tiny Mind. We, like I said, that's me – and, and – yeah, you know. Klas . . . the two of us . . . and you gotta realise – he's a fucking adult, not eight or so. But a grown man, yes he is. And we're – now like totally into this REDNESS, RED ALL OVER. In This – This Here – Totally blood-red Redness. And Then On Top Of That All

The Goo You Get On You The Moment You Get Near The Heart. The Heart-you've-got and the-Heart-I've-got. Oh yeah, Aina! You've got to Realise. It. Aina. That the Two of Us. Klas andMe. We're In It Now. Into Yours – Your Red BUT SOON TO BE – slug-white heart, made of a kind of stuff sort of . . . You know a bit like – rice pudding, sort of. That's just what it looks like now – RICE PUDDING SORT OF BUT RED ALL OVER sor . . . (*Sound of disconnection: click/dead tone.*)

Bibi (*from the sitting-room; offstage*)   Christ, Aina . . . Is he – do you think? – Or was he just having you on?

Now **Inga** *also disappears from the stage; empty for a few seconds.*

Inga (*from the sitting-room; offstage*)   Did you get any sleep?

Bibi (*from the sitting-room; offstage*)   God, you know, I must have . . . I must have done, I suppose.

Aina *comes into the bedroom – and onstage again; she looks perfectly calm, no trace whatever of what has just happened.*

Aina (*on her way into the bedroom*)   Yes, you did . . . you must have done.

Bibi – *dressed now only in white pants and a yellow-green linen nightie with a Mick Jagger portrait on the front – comes onstage with* **Inga**.

The doorbell rings.

Bibi (*startled*)   Oh God . . . it's *him!*

She disappears immediately out of the room – and offstage again; but only for a few seconds – soon she is standing there in the doorway again. She looks imploringly at both **Inga** *and* **Aina** – *who are standing a bit apart from one another, on different sides of the mattresses in the bedroom.*

Bibi (*whispering, a loud whisper*)   Couldn't one of you go?

Aina *then goes – without a word – immediately into the sitting-room offstage . . . Subsequently we can hear 1) her steps out into the hall 2) the opening of the front door 3) low voices out on the stairs and hallway 4) someone coming with* **Aina** *into the flat . . . In the interim:* **Inga**, *leant backwards, with her palms against the window-ledge, looks at*

Bibi – *who* – *casting nervous glances out to the room every now and then – is focusing all her attention there.*

Inga (*smiling amicably, to* **Bibi**)   So you managed to get some sleep anyway?

Gurgle-like 'waking-up sound' from **Erika** *in the cot.* **Inga** *starts; turns round for a second* – *and then once more to* **Bibi**.

(*Now whispering to* **Bibi**.) So you managed to get some sleep anyway?

Bibi (*having cast a hasty glance at* **Inga**)   What? Just wait a moment – quiet!

Aina *and a man come nearer* – *still out in the sitting-room.*

Bibi (*turned away, out to the sitting-room*)   Christ, Paul – you've no idea how much I've been waiting for you.

The sound of **Erika** *in the cot has stopped.*

Aina – *and after her,* **Paul**, *stop beside* **Bibi** *in the doorway* – *they come onstage . . .* **Aina** *and* **Inga** *exchange glances. They both both react at once and in the same way: as though they failed to understand what the other meant but were unable to ask all the same. They turn round several times, questioningly to one another.* **Paul** *and* **Bibi** *hug one another hard.*

Paul (*partly choked by the hug*)   Mmm – Aaah – it – maybe – mm – it's late. Gone a long time – Mmm – Outside – many hours . . . Phew!

Inga *and* **Aina** *look on; both seem a little troubled, now that* **Paul** *and* **Bibi** – *spinning round in an embrace* – *come further and further into the bedroom.*

Paul   When did you get home then?

Bibi   What?

They stop, release one another's arms – **Bibi** *backs away slightly.*

Paul   When did you . . . and Gert – get here then?

Bibi   Oh, I see. Christ. I don't – it was . . . It was ages ago. When – (*Turns to* **Inga**.) Inga – when was it then? It was ages ago.

Aina   Two, three hours ago – something like that? – (*She turns too, after she has answered, to* **Inga** *at the window.*) Isn't that right, Inga?

Inga *has already turned around; opens the blinds – slowly, slowly she turns the blinds: a hint of dawn can be seen out there.*

Bibi (*the whole time looking at* **Paul**)   I . . . Aina told me that you . . . that you went out . . . anyway . . . after us.

Paul   Yes, though . . . I couldn't find you . . . I must – I must have – I must have gone in the wrong direction – you know, when I came out.

Bibi   Yes, I realised that's what you must have done.

Inga *walks over to the doorway; stops there – now that* **Paul** *and* **Bibi** *have ended up there – and, unaware of it, blocks the way.*

Inga   If you wouldn't mind moving, please?

Paul   Oh, of course . . . of course.

Inga (*after a couple of steps into the sitting-room; turns round, looks in at* **Aina** *by* **Erika**'s *cot*)   Aina.

Aina (*whispers, a loud whisper*)   Yes?

Inga (*whispering too, loudly*)   Can I make a call, do you mind?

Aina   Of course you can.

Inga (*whispering, loudly*)   I just thought I'd ring and check if Gert had come home.

She disappears out into the sitting-room – and offstage; we hear her telephoning out there, dialling etc.

Bibi (*in a normal voice, which now sounds loud*)   No, you see, about Gert . . . Well, he – You, you know, after about an hour I left him on his own. He hasn't come back yet.

Paul (*speaking suddenly almost even louder than* **Bibi**)   So you – the two of you didn't come back here together then? – No, I see, I see.

Bibi   He went straight home – that's what Inga thought –
to their flat in town.

Aina   Shuush!

Aina *tries to hear to whether* **Inga** *is talking out there in the sitting-
room offstage –* **Gert** *does seem to have answered. But* **Inga** *is talking
too softly to hear any words.*

Aina   Well, he's – Gert's – definitely home now anyway.

Aina *disappears into the sitting-room as well, offstage.*

Paul   What did happen?

Bibi   Oh, you know, he wanted – he just *had* to take me to –
a sort of park area, which is nearby, if you – well, if you sort of
continue on . . . Past, you know, this row and all those houses
which looked – that's what I thought at the time – brown
when we arrived, but which are actually more sort of
reddish, more kind of pale red sort of. You know the ones I
mean.

Paul   The ones like we're in now you mean? Yes, I see. This
row of houses.

Bibi   Yes . . . down as far as . . . well, actually, they looked
brown as well, when we arrived – but they're . . . more
greenish sort of, once you get closer . . . Do you know which
ones I mean? It doesn't really matter. Well, opposite them
more or less . . . there's a sort of park. And we were supposed
to go in there. He was absolutely determined to show me
what was in there – and – then, you see, it turned out to be –
just a – all it was – just a small, roughly my size – although
very true to life, skilfully done bronze sculpture – of a –
perfectly ordinary, rather pretty – young girl.

Paul   What, in the park?

Bibi   Well, yes, right there in the middle . . . And then, well
then. That's when he wanted to tell me. What it was about it
. . . you know, that was so important. The reason why we
were there in the first place –

*Stops, looks down. Then looks up again – with a little smile – at **Paul**; she continues when he doesn't interrupt; instead he looks almost curious.*

He'd – it turned out that – he'd lived in this very area, round about five years ago. He was living with a – a Belgian, a woman from Belgium then . . . he had met on some business journey down in Brussels. The way I heard it, Gert has got one, or maybe two, sweetshops, in the city. Although, as he said, he has been dealing in chocolate and sweets, as a wholesaler – for, I don't know, ten, fifteen years . . . That last year, he was living – *out here*, you see – with that woman from Brussels. And that was when he used to pass by that bronze sculpture in the park, every evening mostly. He had to go for a walk in order to be able to fall asleep. And then one night, in the middle of winter at Christmas time. Well, it was completely desolate out here. Totally silent. And then suddenly he just lost it, sort of – completely lost his mind. Pulled down his trousers. And, well . . . started to *masturbate*. In front of the bronze girl!

*Once again, gurgling sounds from the cot. Both **Paul** and **Bibi** turn around, walk cautiously over; they look, both of them, down at her . . . In the background: the murmuring of **Inga**'s conversation.*

Bibi   God, she's so lovely.

Paul   And you mean that was *it?* – the thing he absolutely had to show you? Go out for a walk, just to show you a sculpture.

Bibi   I don't know, I've got no idea what he planned. But, well, it must have been, I suppose . . . what . . . he said, that afterwards, he'd – well, sort of imagined he heard something, in the bushes. Someone, you see, could have been there and seen him, with his trousers down, in front of that girl sculpture – she had – that's what struck me when I was standing there – such terribly empty, dark bronze eyes, and then, there was the fact that it's always standing there, standing there among the trees for ever and ever. That's all he wanted to show me. That's when I left – I felt I had to. Gert was standing there looking at her. And he said sort of – 'This is my punishment. That she's – the girl's – always here'

. . . It just felt a bit sick. (*Suddenly looks as though she is going to cry.*) And then when I got here . . . to the road, I mean . . . the one that runs past this house . . . It was at a – at a corner, sort of. (*Leant forward now, her palms against her knees.*)

Paul   What was it? What happened then? Bibi? What was it?

Bibi *gets up; breathes in – deeply – several times . . . And then takes five or six paces away from* **Paul** *at the cot – breathing very heavily the whole time – her hands pressed now – as she leans forward again – tightly against her knees . . . Close to tears: breathing . . .*

Bibi   Just when I got to the middle of the street – well, that's when it appeared – I mean . . . I think, I think – it was a – one of those, you know, newspaper vans, that . . . uhm, you know – that –

Paul   That deliver the morning papers?

Bibi   Yes – and I was sort of – well, I was nearly run over.

She stretches again . . . But now she begins to shake – as though she were incredibly cold – out in a freezing wind.

(*In a delicate almost baby voice.*)   Paul . . . I – got so . . . I got so – dreadfully scared.

Paul *goes over to* **Bibi***; embraces her tighter and tighter . . . as though to warm her, he kneads his palms quickly over her back.*

Paul   It's all over now, Bibi. The danger's over now . . .

Suddenly **Bibi** *SCREAMS.* **Paul** *releases her – distressed; looks at her. Once more: she SCREAMS STRAIGHT OUT again.*

In the silence a third gurgle-sound from the cot.

Aina *with a little bunch of grapes – and* **Inga** *with the receiver in her hands, peer in from the other room:* **Paul** *takes the handkerchief from his pocket and offers it. All three of them look on, in astonishment, at* **Bibi**.

Bibi   Just got so, I just got so – when it was coming, you see. The truck . . . when it was coming . . . Got so . . . scared . . . Christ!

Inga *in the middle of her unfinished telephone conversation disappears – offstage.*

Paul   Bibi, here's my handkerkchief. It's a bit used . . . But only a bit.

Bibi *now on her way out,* **Paul** *follows; both pass* **Aina** *at the door. She is eating a grape, glances at* **Erika**, *who has fallen silent . . . Then* **Aina** *turns off her bedside lamp; leaves the stage – the last to do so.*

Next second: The stage in total darkness.

The Gate Theatre presents the British Premiere of

The Oginski Polonaise

by Nikolai Kolyada

translated by Peter Tegel

cast

David	Tony Cealy
Dima	Ged McKenna
Ludmila	Pam Merrick
Ivan	Mario Vernazza
Tanya	Victoria Worsley
Sergei	Jez Zeke

Director	Pat Kiernan
Designer	Helen Evans
Lighting Designer	Richard Johnson
Sound Designer	Cormec O'Connor
Production Manager	Vian Curtis
Stage Manager	Dominic Bristow
Deputy Stage Manager	Caron Lyon
Assistant Designer	Michael Coles
Assistant Production Manager	Charlotte Hall
Assistant Stage Manager	Abi Coyle

for the Biennale

Artistic Director	David Farr
Producer	Rose Garnett
Project Co-ordinator	Clare Goddard
Manager	Karen Hopkins
Literary Supervisor	Joy Lo Dico
Production Co-ordinator	Melissa Naylor
Press Officer	Rachel Stafford

Pat Kiernan was the runner up for the 1995 Karabé Award donated by Jenny Hall.

With thanks to the Arts Council and to Tanya Nesterova for her help with the text.

Biographies

Dominic Bristow (Stage Manager)
Trained at ARTTS International. Work includes DSM on **South Pacific** (Drill Hall), DSM on **The Isle of the Departed** (Man in The Moon), ASM on **Agamemnon's Children** (Gate). Member of the technical crew at the Pleasance during the Edinburgh Festival in 1994 and 1995.

Tony Cealy (David)
Started his career as a film actor. He has appeared in over thirty films, **The Collector** (Channel 4) and **There'll be Tears Before Bedtime** both reached the London Film Festival. As well as teaching film-making he is a member of Tellers Theatre, whose improvised shows have toured prisons and hospitals up and down the country. He has just finished directing Jean Cocteau's **The Sound of Silence** at the Baron Court and will be playing the lead in Channel 4's gritty drama **Mirrors and Memoirs** (Black Pyramid Films).

Michael Coles (Assistant Designer)
Trained in Theatre Technical Arts: Design at Wimbledon School of Arts. He has created the lighting for productions as diverse as **Ghost**, **Lock up Your Daughters**, **The Glass Menagerie** and the Windsor Jazz Festival together with the setting for a presentation of Chaucer's **The Miller's Tale**. He is a Diploma Member of the Chartered Society of Designers.

Abi Coyle (Assistant Stage Manager)
Abi graduated from the BRIT School in July 1995. Since then she has worked on four Steam Industry productions: **Dracula** (BAC and Regent's Park), **Venom** (Drill Hall), **The Hired Man** (Finborough) and **South Pacific** (Drill Hall).

Vian Curtis (Production Manager)
Resident Production Manager at the Gate. Trained at RADA. Theatre includes **Bloodknot** and **Don Juan Comes Back From the War** (Gate), **Heart and Sole** (Gilded Balloon/Newcastle Comedy Festival), **So You Think You're Funny?!** (Gilded Balloon), **The Lottery Ticket** (BAC and Pleasance), carpenter for Hilton Productions and **Miss Julie** (New End Theatre, Hampstead).

Helen Evans (Designer)
Trained at Wimbledon's School of Art in Technical Arts: Design, graduated 1995. Theatre includes **Voices** (Royal Court Young People's Theatre), **160th Anniversary Weekend** (Welfare State International), **Silverface** and **Ballad of Wolves** (Gate).

Charlotte Hall (Assistant Production Manager)
Trained at Aberystwyth University. Theatre includes publicity team member for the National Student Theatre Company (Edinburgh '94), Company Manager for the National Student Theatre Company (Edinburgh '95), Deputy Stage Manager **Silverface** (Gate), Stage Manager for **Dracula** (Steam Industry at BAC), **Cat and Mouse (Sheep)** and **Services** (Gate).

Richard Johnson (Lighting Designer)
Theatre includes **Fear and Loathing in Las Vegas** (Gate and Fortune Theatre), **Beyond Therapy** directed by Tom Conti, **Down and Out in London and Paris**, **Savage in Limbo**, **Naomi**, **His Lordship's Fancy** and **Amphitryon** (Gate), **Loot** directed by Kenneth Williams (Arts Theatre), Ken Hill's **Phantom of the Opera** (Newcastle Playhouse), **Onnagata** (Lindsay Kemp World Tour), **900 Oneonta** (Lyric Hammersmith), **Borders of Paradise** (Watford Palace) and **A Clockwork Orange** (Newcastle Playhouse).

Pat Kiernan (Director)
Awarded best director at the Irish Student Drama Festival 1990. Founded Corcadorca Theatre Company in 1991. Work with the company includes **Leonce and Lena**, **That Scoundrel Scapin**, **Rave to Real**, **The Love of Don Perlimplin**, **The Ginger Ale Boy** and **A Clockwork Orange**. With Feedback Theatre Company, Thomas Kilroy's **Talbot's Box**. The Arts Council of Ireland awarded Pat the 1994 President Robinson Goodman Theatre Chicago Fellowship and he was runner up for the Karabé Award 1995.

Nikolai Kolyada (Writer)
At thirty-eight, Nikolai Kolyada is currently the most performed playwright of his generation in Russia, with sixteen of his thirty-seven plays in the repertoires of 150 theatres. Born in Kazakhastan, he has made his home in Ekaterinburg, the former 'closed' city of Sverdlovsk in Asian Russia where the Tsar was killed and where Yeltsin was once Communist party chief. At the age of fifteen Kolyada entered Sverdlosk Theatre School and on completion worked for seven years as an actor at Sverdlosk Academi Theatre.

Kolyada wrote his first play, **Forfeits**, in 1986 and by 1989 was accepted into the USSR Writers Union. Since then his work has included **The Catapult** (1989), **The Fairy Tale of the Dead Tsareuna, a farce for adults** (1990), **The American** (1991) and **Kanotype** (1992). He is not married but has four cats and a tortoise.

Caron Lyon (Deputy Stage Manager)

Caron has come to the Gate after a gruelling panto season at Derby Playhouse. Before that Caron was Stage Manager for Forest Forge Theatre Company and has spent several months at Butlins as their Stage Manager and general dog's body!! She is thrilled to be here at the Gate and hopes to survive the London experience which she is new to.

Ged McKenna (Dima)

Trained at Central. Most recently he worked for Shared Experience in Polly Teale's production of **Desire Under the Elms**, previous theatre work includes **Macbeth** (Cheek By Jowl), **The Shaughraun**, **Bartholomew Fair**, **Ghetto** (NT), **From This Day Forward** (WAT), **Divine Words** (BAC) **A House by the Sea** (BAC), **The Dancing Room** (Wookey Hole Caves), **Romeo and Juliette** (Canizarro Park). He has played the title roles in both **Macbeth** and **Woyzeck** for Astra Theatre at the Dock. TV/Filmwork includes **Rockliffe's Babies**, **Boon**, **The Paradise Club**, **The Long Roads** (Screen 2) and **Shirley Valentine** (Paramount). He is also a writer and his latest play, **The Farmer's Bride**, is due for production by Wild Iris in the autumn.

Pam Merrick (Ludmila)

West End: Ruth in **Night and Day** (Phoenix), Lady Joan in **Last of Mrs Cheyney** (Cambridge), Lydia in **All My Sons** (Wyndham's) and Mama in **Shayna Maidel** (Ambassadors). TV includes Hortense in **Bleak House**, **Casualty**, **Eastenders**, **Tenko** and **Unsolved Mysteries**. Fringe: Joan in **Sexual Perversity** (Man in the Moon), Madeleine 1 in **The Real World** (Soho Poly), title role in **Phaedra** (Pentameters), Aisinoe and director **The Misanthrope** (Pentameters), Madam Walter in **The Sensualist** (Arts Theatre). Rep: Richmond, Derby, Century, Watford, Swansea, Folkstone. Favourite role is Martha in **Who's Afraid of Virginia Woolf**.

Cormec O'Connor (Sound Designer)
This is Cormec's first show outside his native Ireland. Hailing from an Indie-pop background, in 1995 he designed the sound for **A Clockwork Orange**, Arthur Miller's **A View from the Bridge**, **The Rock Station** by Ger Fitzgibbon and **The Ginger Ale Boy** by Enda Walsh. After **The Oginski Polonaise** he will return to Ireland to start work on Corcadorca's production of **Animal Farm**.

Peter Tegel (Translator)
As a playwright, plays include **Blim at School**, **Poet of the Anemones** (Royal Court Theatre Upstairs) and numerous radio plays, the most recent being **Happy Depths of a Homophobe** with Derek Jacobi (Radio 3, 1993). Translations from Russian include **The Suicide** by Nikolai Erdman (RSC, Radio 3), **Strider** by Rozovsky based on Tolstoy's story (NT), **Shooting Ducks** by Vampilov (Radio 3 and Theatre Royal, Stratford East), **The Mandate** by Nikolai Erdman (Radio 3 and New End Theatre), **5 Songs in an Old House** by Arro (Radio 3). In 1992 he was awarded an Arts Council grant to translate Nikolai Kolyada's play, **The Catapult**.

Mario Vernazza (Ivan)
Trained at Rose Bruford and studied commedia dell'arte in Italy with Antonio Fava. Theatre work includes a national tour with **The Red Princess** (Red Shift), **Dance Baby Diddy** (Chelsea Centre), **Othello** (European tour) and **The Hour Between Dog and Wolf** (Lilian Baylis Theatre).

Victoria Worsley (Tanya)
Theatre includes **Night Train**, Jade/Belgrade, Coventry co-production (Lyric Hammersmith and Belgrade), **The Thirst** (Leicester Haymarket), **Grapes of Wrath**, **Nervous Women**, **Turn of the Screw** (Birmingham Rep), **Prin**, **Don Carlos** (Lyric Hammersmith), **Macbeth** (Ludlow Festival), **Wardance** (Lumiere and Son), **Make Me a Statue** (ICA). Founded companies: Tattycoram and Jade. TV/Film includes **Archers Goon** (BBC), **Prisoners of Honour** (Warner Bros) and **South by South East** (ITV).

Jez Zeke (Sergei)
Television: over twenty productions including **Boon**, **Casualty**, **The Chronicles of Narnia**, **The One Game** and **The Bill**. He has appeared in two full-length and several short films and numerous plays in the theatre. During the past twelve months he

has played Walter Ormund in Priestley's **I Have Been Before**, Frank in Brian Friel's **Faith Healer** and recently a tour of England as Frank in **Educating Rita**. He made a short film last summer with Paul McGann (due to be released this autumn) and starred in the short film, **Animal**, screened on Channel 4 last autumn.

The Oginski Polonaise

Nikolai Kolyada
Translation by Peter Tegel

Characters

Tanya, *thirty*
Dima, *thirty*
Ivan, *forty*
Ludmila, *forty*
Sergei, *forty-five*
David, *thirty*

Setting
Winter, January. The present. A three-room flat in an old building in the centre of Moscow.

Note
This text went to press before the opening night and may therefore differ from the version as performed.

Act One

... the street, the street, the street. I'm walking. Looking
down at the tarmac. Daytime, wind, sun, cold. I can look at
the tarmac but not the faces. Nobody in this town knows me
and I know no one. No one. No one. I'll meet no one, greet no
one, kiss no one ('Hello! How are you then?'). No. There'll be
no meetings. I don't want to meet anyone. I don't need to.
Because inside me with me is my world where there are people
to meet, to greet, to kiss ('Hello! How are you then?').
Myworld. Myworld. Mine. MYWORLD. MY-WORLD.

It's not town and not countryside, not sea and not land, not
forest and not field, but forest and field, and sea, and land, and
town, and countryside – my world. MINE. A WORLD.

Like my world or not, it makes no difference to me. Because *I*
like MY WORLD – I love it.

In My World there are streets I know in every detail, roads
and paths I've taken a hundred times, narrow quiet
alleyways, windows, houses, there's day and night, night and
day. There's my past, future and present all in one, right here,
right now, not flowing, not spilling into each other. And
there's you. You.

In this World of mine there's winter, summer, spring, autumn
– yes, there's my beloved, my rainswept autumn, the autumn
no one loves: with yellow leaves in black frozen puddles;
autumn in my world takes up a lot of space, much more than
in yours, in your world, in yours ...

There are people in my world, many: those I love, those close
to me, cherished. They live in My World because they
stepped into it. They all met me by chance, but I know I had
to bump into them one day and take them into my world, My
World, MINE. Otherwise there'd be blank spaces in my
world: flats no one moved into, empty streets, envelopes
without letters inside, ringing phones and no one speaking.

In my world there are people like cats and cats like people: I call the cats Vasya, Bageera, Shnurok, Shishok and Manyura, little Manyura. There are stray dogs I picked up on the street – your street, yours – picked up and took into my world, MY WORLD. There's Sharik the dog and the cat Tshapa (they lived with Sonya), died, and I took them into my world, MY WORLD; did it because there was nowhere else for them to go and now they live in My World; I've taken many people who died into my world, MY WORLD, forgotten by everyone but in My World they're alive – they live! There are also two tortoises in my world (one from my childhood, nameless, I've forgotten its name, and the other – Manya, poor Manya). Also from my childhood Zorka the cow – big, white, good-natured, with big black eyes, and Zorka's right horn was broken . . .

And there's a big lake, frozen right through in the winter; in my childhood which is also in My World, I go to school over the ice in a snowstorm – so often I go, so often: every night, every night, every night, every . . . There's a little house at the edge of Pryesnogorkovka: the house has a roof of red tin, from the roof I can see a forest, a field, a road, the sky, I see and I dream of countries far away. There are countries far away in my world: there are palm trees and the sea, aeroplanes and hotels, and melodious foreign languages. And in this World of Mine there is God, MY GOD, not yours; the God I invented and to whom I always talk all the time; and there's a church – my church, where Father Gleb says Mass; and there's a cemetery – it grows larger every day; there's mother, father, there's Nadya, Vera, Andrei and Vovka, there's also Sergei, not separate, together; and there's old Shura (just last night I ran into her again – I was carrying a bag of flour – ran into her), smiling from under her glasses she said: 'Bring me at least, at least five bottles of beer . . .', looked at me carefully, shut the red door of the hostel and quietly went away – but I saw, I saw: there, there behind the red door it was dark as pitch, night . . .

How big, how big it is! How big you are – MY WORLD. Alive because I'm alive and you'll die with me, when I die.

Forgive me, but for you I found no place in My World: your
features slowly melted, distance and time (medicine, my
medicine in My World!) effaced the colour photo and with it
your smile and your eyes, only your hands remain; I dream of
them sometimes, or rather, their outlines, but you – you're
not here: the places are taken, all taken and there's still plenty
of people who'd like to get into My World, and perhaps I'll let
them; but you – you won't be on the roads I take, I don't want
it and that's all there is to it: one shouldn't lie, it's a sin, but –
hush, no need to remember everything – here's the way, this
way, here . . .

Wait, wait . . . just a little more, a tiny bit . . . The transfer on
the old fissured wall of the house of My World sends out a
milky white film, full of bubbles – colours are getting brighter,
outlines arising everywhere, colour and light, yes, yes –
already quite clear! – the moment's fiery light has arrived, has
paused right here, has entered MY WORLD: the empty
space has filled, everything has found its place and now, only
now do I understand that this picture and these people were
always with me, but they took their time before they began to
disturb me with their talk, they waited listening – the present
is always taciturn and quiet – now the Time has come, they've
come to life, they walk along the streets of MY INVENTED
WORLD,
of MY WORLD,
of the WORLD . . .

Scene One

The flat.

*There are signs of former wealth in the three-room flat in the centre of
Moscow: the stucco work on the ceiling, the high doors with antique
handles; the luxurious lamp with the green shade – which is in the largest
room, the living-room; the tall mirror in the corridor; the chair by the
table in the kitchen – an old-fashioned, massive leather chair; the hall-
stand by the front door – a stand on bentwood legs.*

Mixed with the flat's old furniture are simple cheap Soviet tables and chairs. The rooms are spacious, they can't be crammed full, no matter how hard the flat's inhabitants try.

Dima*'s room is to the left of the front door: the room is incredibly filthy and dusty. There's a bed by the balcony door, or rather, a wire mesh on books. In a corner there's a pile of paper and envelopes. The balcony is wide with old cast-iron railings. In the distance, the red lights of the Ostankino Television Tower blink in the dusk.*

Ivan*'s room is to the right of the front door. There's a table, a sofa, television and a cupboard. In the corner by the window a palm in a blue plastic tub.*

The corridor leads to the door of **Ludmila***'s and* **Sergei***'s room. The lamp and some completely useless furniture are here – chairs, little cupboards, two tables, a desk, a large dresser. A wide bed stands in the centre of the room under the lamp.*

There are three doors halfway down the corridor: to the lavatory, the bathroom and the kitchen. The kitchen has a large window and a gas cooker. There are boxes, jars, bags, empty bottles everywhere. Wine and vodka labels are pasted on one of the walls right to the ceiling. A home-made curtain of strung corks hangs in the doorway.

In the corridor, to the right of the front door, hangs a cuckoo clock. The corridor walls and ceiling are decorated with a New Year set of lights that keeps flashing.

On some carpet in the corridor by the front door sits a goose. Next to it, a plate with soaked bread and a tin with water. Now and then the goose rises up and, replying to the cuckoo clock, lets out a thin and cracked cry, and beats its wings as if trying to fly. Then it sits down again and keeps quiet.

Perhaps because the flat is in the very centre of Moscow, the restless sounds of the city at night carry here constantly: music from restaurants, the babble of television, the roar of planes. Overlaying these sounds comes the siren, aggressive and spiteful, of an ambulance as it approaches, then draws away.

The corridor.

Sitting on the floor by the goose and hugging his knees is **Ivan**. **Sergei** *is on a stool by the mirror. He wears track suit trousers, a vest and slippers. He is eating soup slowly and with relish, holding the plate in his hands. Opposite him like his reflection — also on a stool and also with a plate in her hands — sits* **Ludmila**. *She smokes as she eats, inhaling deeply.*

The faces of those sitting in the corridor are lit, now red, then blue, then green by the set of lights.

Ludmila *and* **Sergei** *are silent for a long while.* **Ivan** *seems to be crying.*

Ivan (*puts a finger to his forehead, 'shoots'*)   Bam, bam, bam, bam . . .

Ludmila   God knows how she got stuck into astrology! She could have lived here. No, she has to move out. She wrote novels, stories. Naturally I never got to see them. She hid them. As for music. Classical. She could play. She worked at it. She taught herself. My daughter! A golden girl. A writer. Was. Out of the blue she gets stuck into astrology. She could even draw. We had friends in Germany, German friends, Dresden, engineers, him and her, they knew about culture. Brilliant, they said she was, brilliant . . .

Sergei (*eating*)   Brilliant balls!

Ludmila   She's not your daughter, so you're angry. (*Falls silent, eats soup, smokes.*) Brilliant is what they said. Only now she's stuck into astrology. What for, don't ask me! She's stuck in it and that's all there is to it. It's all she thinks about now, astrology. Mind you, there's something out there, I believe that. I wear a cross. Just in case. My mother, she always said: God exists, and if he doesn't, let him be. We had a church in our village, I went when I was little. Brilliant, they said it, brilliant. (*Pause.*) Leaves me and goes to Ulan Ude, and why? Because, according to her, they have a different meridian out there. That's right, a different meridian, so now she's stuck even deeper in astrology.

Sergei   Into shitology. She's soft in the head, your daughter. She buggered off to get away from you.

Ludmila   Keep quiet and pay attention when you're eating. Or your food'll go down the wrong way and you'll croak. Like it?

Sergei   My favourite, smoked flies, fried worms and shit pies. Washed down with warm piss, bliss! (*Laughs, guffaws, eats.*)

Silence.

Ludmila   If I'd not worked all my life as a presser in our factory, I'd have written novels. A writer, that's what I'd have been, or a painter. A writer. I'd have published in Dresden, or in the West somewhere. I always felt I had the talent. 'Who's going to be Father Frost at the factory nursery this New Year?' the foreman would ask at meetings. They'd point to me: her! Three glasses of vodka and I was off, Father Frost at your service! Very jolly I was, very witty and comical. The children rolled about laughing because of me. When I get a pension I'm writing a novel about my destiny, all the unhappiness and the bitterness, all that went wrong in my life, everything that was plain negative . . . (*Wipes away her tears.*)

Silence.

Ivan (*puts a finger to his temple*)   Bam, bam, bam . . . (*Falls silent.*) Has her plane landed yet?

Pause. The siren outside the window. The cuckoo comes out, calls eight times. The goose wakes up, cries twice.

(*To himself.*) It's landed. She'll be here soon.

Ludmila   Maybe it crashed?

Ivan   Eh?

Ludmila *puts the plate on the floor, goes to the phone, wipes her hands on her dress, dials, bites her lip, asks:*

Ludmila   Could you tell me please? The New York-Moscow flight, has it crashed? Or did it land? (*Listens.*) Stupid cow!

She puts down the receiver, paces the corridor. Lights another cigarette.

Ivan   End of the *dolce vita*. What else? Crashed. You and Sergei always want to have your cake and eat it. (*'Shoots' himself in the forehead.*) Bam, bam, bam ...

Silence.

Ludmila, lend me some money.

Ludmila   I don't have money to lend. I don't lend money to anyone. And I wouldn't lend money to you of all people because you never pay it back.

Silence.

Ivan (*'shoots'*)   Bam, bam, bam ... (*Pause.*) Sergei doesn't smoke, but he looks like a smoker, so you want to ask him for a cigarette. You look like a money-lender, Ludmila, but you don't have and you don't give.

Ludmila   Dead right. There's no one poorer. (*Pause.*) Wish I was a millionairess's lapdog, there in the West. Slips on her mink and goes walkies, me behind her, hop skip over the marble steps. I'd piddle, do a heap, she'd pick me up and give me a hug, we'd both be happy. At home I'd go to my bowl and stuff myself, then to my basket. And sleep and sleep and sleep and dream of bones and lick my lips. I die of envy when I see those whoring bitch millionairesses on television. Why, I want to know, was I not born a dog in a rich whore's home, why? Sergei, why? Have you had enough? Have some more pie, it's fresh, and drink up your tea.

Sergei   Eat tea, drink pie. Pee. (*Laughs.*) I don't feel so good. Lenin's dead, Stalin's dead and I'm taking a turn for the worse. (*Guffaws.*) I fancy something sour.

Ludmila   You fancy, you'll stop fancying. Mama says no. (*Sits down, eats soup, smokes.*) She'll be here in a minute, watch her jaw drop! You'll get something sour then all right, we all will, smack in the face. I can hear her already: Where are my things, where are they?

Sergei   Moscow crows straight from fucking Papua.

Ivan   Bam, bam, bam, bam, bam, bam ...

Ludmila   A bird on the wing, that's me, a lifetime living out of suitcases, clutching all I own, all for the sake of living in bloody Moscow, all just so as not to have to go back. A life lived in dread that she'll be back, she'll throw us out.

Ivan   What stopped her coming back sooner?

Ludmila   It hurt the girl to pay, or she'd have come. Now she needs to sell the flat. And throw us out. And that's it!

Ivan   Bitter grief roamed the world and chanced upon us here. Bam!

Sergei   Shat upon us here. (*Guffaws.*)

Ivan (*silent*)   Say what you like, I'm not sleeping in the corridor. Why should I? First the corridor, then you'll shove me onto the landing. I can just hear it: 'Vanya, well, he's not Kaltenbrunner, he's not Schnitzelblum, he's not Barenboim, so let him sleep out on the street.' Russians are being discriminated against worldwide. I show films like that all the time now. That's how it is. Besides, I know you, Ludmila. You'll come to an arrangement with her fast enough, you'll lick her arse. Yours is the biggest room, you and Sergei sleep in the corridor. Or let her. Doesn't bother me. If it's for only two weeks, she can. Provided she doesn't worm her way in, it's our life here, not hers. This is our country! We live here!

Sergei (*eating*)   We shit here. And it's not for two weeks, she's coming back for good. A new life, is what she said. I shall make a fresh start.

Ludmila   Ten years we've lived here, what, and now sleep in the corridor? Up yours, Ivan! Up yours!

Ivan   I've lived here ten years too, so? What of it?

Silence.

The set of lights flash. Faces are lit blue, red, yellow. Outside the window a siren wails. The cuckoo replies to the siren, the goose to the cuckoo.

Ludmila (*paces the corridor, swings her arms, sings quietly and angrily*)   'You failed to understand my love! It was wasted! Wa-aa-sted! A rainbow over the fields! It glowed! It went out!' (*Pause.*) A new life! The cheek! The effin cheek! As if the old one weren't good enough! When we just about deliberately sell her furniture and all her junk so as not to be reminded of that family, here she is. Lovely to see you again! Oh, is she going to be furious! Is she going to yell! We're knee deep in it! Any minute now!

Sergei   What's worse than an uninvited guest? A Tartar. What's better than an uninvited guest? A Tartar. (*Laughs.*) A joke. A jo-ooke.

Ludmila   Brainless clot with your stupid answers for everything! The responsibility as always lands smack on my frail shoulders. Ha ha! He he! That's you! We have nothing. We're barefoot beggars and she's in leather. Wait till she arrives, you'll see how she's dressed. If she even thinks of giving me one of her old cast-off coats, please God she brings one, it'll be my Sunday best.

Ivan (*'shoots'*)   Bam, bam, bam, bam . . .

Ludmila (*to her husband*)   Don't whinge! He sits there chomping.

The goose gets up, calls three times.

Ivan   I dreamed about borsch today. Red borsch. I was spooning it in. And suddenly I see it's got hair in it. Fine black hair. And I'm picking them out one by one off the plate, the spoon. It set me thinking about my village . . .

Sergei   Sewage, more like. No matter which way you piss, the last drop ends in your trousers. (*Guffaws.*)

Ludmila   Village, village! The same old tune on the old broken balalaika. I sing what I see: a plank and a rope and I'm lord of the land. For ten years he's chewed my ears off with his village. I come from a village, I do my very best to forget those bleak years of my life. Go on, clear off back to your village if you're that homesick for hairy borsch, clear off! There'll be room for her then. Clear off!

Ivan (*shouts*)   It's not my fault I live here! Or that my life's a mess! Leave my village alone! It's not my fault I'm Ivan, and

not Schnitzelblum, not Kaltenbrunner! You've no
conscience, you and Sergei. You've torn yourselves up by the
roots, you've forgotten where you come from! Keep out of my
life!

He cries, his face buried between his knees. Is silent for a while. **Sergei**
eats. **Ludmila** *paces the corridor.*

Ludmila   Don't ask me why she got stuck in astrology.

Ivan   Hair, full of hair. Bam, bam, bam, bam . . .

Sergei (*laughs*)   They have shops signs abroad in Russian
for tourists and immigrants from Russia: 'Unlimited supply
of shit for sale.' I swear it, my boss told me, he's there often.
Shopfuls of shit, as much as you want. Cheap too. In bulk.
(*Hiccups.*) Who's thinking of me then?

Ludmila   They have fantastic chewing gum. Maybe she'll
bring us some.

Sergei   You won't get any. Shit is what she'll bring us.

Ludmila   You're right, I've got this false impression of
quality in the West. I picked up five pairs of knickers two
months ago, in a set. Knickers, well, Sergei's seen them, they
had this little man on them, right in the centre, a little man in
a boat. What happens? I wear them once, kaput. So now I use
my knickers to wipe the kitchen table.

Sergei   Women's?

Ludmila   What?

Sergei   Knickers?

Ludmila   Do I look like I go around in men's knickers?

Ivan ('*shoots*')   Bam, bam, bam, bam, bam . . .

Again the siren, the cuckoo, the goose: all loud together at the same time.
Pause.

Sergei (*hiccups*)   Who's thinking about me then?

Ludmila   I can't wait to cut that stupid goose's throat. Oi
yoi yoi . . . Farewell, unwashed Russia, land where only slaves
and masters dwell. Tara-lala a uniform tara-lala!

Sergei   Eh?

Ludmila   Esenin said it. Farewell, unwashed Russia, land where only slaves and masters dwell. I know heaps of poetry from school, we had a Russian teacher in our village. Here's another, same idea, same mood. Only remember the last verse though: 'Don't look so eagerly at the road! Oblivion's what I want, and sleep!' (*Weeps.*)

Sergei (*laughs*)   Kiss her melon bum! Bloody rubbish!

Ivan   Farewell, unwashed Russia . . .

Sergei   Farewell, unwashed Russia . . .

Ivan (*cries*)   Farewell, unwashed Russia . . .

Ludmila   Farewell, unwashed Russia . . . (*Pause.*) Where are we off to anyway? We're ending our days here. So why say goodbye?

Ivan   What's she need the entire flat for to herself? She'll fit in the corridor. I remember her, skinny.

Ludmila   Was. She's probably put on weight. Where she's coming from sausages drop out of the sky.

Sergei (*hiccups*)   Who's thinking of me then?

Ivan   A new life! What if she means it? Eh? What happens then?

Sergei (*laughs helplessly*)   We're in dogshit, but for real.

Ivan   What then?

Ludmila   We'll just have to drop our load on the street.

Sergei   She'll sell the flat to some little shitty pants, a Jap or a Chink. That's what they all do. (*Guffaws.*) Sell and leave, sell and leave . . .

Ludmila (*angry*)   You're like them on bloody television talking about prices going up on basic commodities. That's how they sound. Hasn't it sunk in? We'll be on the street like strays, pissing under bridges. That's where we'll be living, under bridges!

Ivan At the cinema yesterday somebody said to me: 'We're strangers here at this festival of life.'

Ludmila He was right. Farewell, unwashed Russia. Oh farewell, unwashed . . .

Ivan Farewell, unwashed Russia . . .

Sergei (*echoing*) Farewell, unwashed Russia.

Ludmila New Year was a hundred years ago, he still hasn't taken down his lights. This flashing is getting on my nerves.

Sergei It's gorgeous. Like a monkey's arse.

Ludmila My eyes hurt.

Sergei Your eyes aren't your bum, put your finger in and get it out. (*Guffaws.*)

Ludmila That's enough for one day! You're in for it with your jokes.

Sergei Not all is for the greater glory of God.

Ivan Dima left the lights up so it's cheerful. It's his birthday in a week.

Ludmila Cyclops has a birthday! Fuck me, said the elephant when he shat in the bath! So he's got a birthday! All his life he pours it in for no good reason, lo and behold, now there's a festive occasion, a birthday, now he's got a reason! You encourage him, you drink with him, you and Sergei, he pays. Sergei, why could you not say when she phoned: 'Moscow has had an earthquake, the house has burned down! A gale blew off the roof! Nowhere to stay stop sleeping in ditches stop send financial help stop Sergei!' Why wasn't I in when she phoned, I'd have told her, but you – eugh! I'd have faxed her all the way to her rotten stinking America!

Sergei We don't have a fax.

Ludmila Keep quiet, you moron! We'd have found one for this! Why didn't I think of it before!

Sergei Why didn't you shit on the floor? Good ideas always come late. (*Hiccups.*) Who's thinking of me then, Ludmila?

Silence.

Ivan   If I had the money I'd buy a flat in Moscow and live here.

Ludmila   If he had the money he'd buy a flat.

Ivan   Why am I Vanya? Why am I not Kaltenbrunner?

Ludmila   She'll be here any minute, and she'll be asking: 'Where are my things?'

Sergei   We'll tell her: 'Down the hatch! Up the chimney!'

Ivan   Where? Furniture, beds, sofas, carpets. Vanished!

Ludmila   Beds, sofas, carpets! What a whinger!

Sergei   What's she been doing there for ten years?

Ludmila   What do you think? It's the same for women the world over. Abroad, she's still a woman: no real support. What else could she do? The devil must have got your tongue, Sergei, to make you say to her: 'Come!' I'd have said right into the phone: 'Fuck off, don't set foot! We've buried you!' You stupid turd, Sergei! Tomorrow I'm going to church, I'm putting a candle out for her, on its head, upside down, so she'll clear off after two days back to her America! God, why did I profuckingcrastinate, fool, I should have done it sooner! She'll throw us out, Sergei, out, did you hear, out!

She sobs. The goose cries.

Sergei   No panic on the Titanic.

Ivan   Belt up, Sergei.

Ludmila   Belt up, Sergei!

Sergei (*suddenly gets up, strikes the wall with his spoon, angry*) Sergei, shit! I've had enough! Nothing suits you. One minute your arse is too cold, the next the radiator's too hot! I'm sick of it. I cheer you up, I'm funny all evening, I make the best jokes I can think of! What do I get? Sergei, Sergei! I'm fed up! You're the morons! I can't get a word in. I'm also . . . I mean, me, I'm also . . . I'm . . .

Suddenly bursts into tears, goes to the lavatory, slams the door.

Ludmila *starts to sob hysterically, goes to the kitchen, sits at the table, her head in her hands.*

Ivan *leaps up from the floor, goes to the bathroom, washes, weeps.*

Silence.

A key turns in the lock on the front door. The door opens. **Tanya** *enters. She wears a dress resembling a tutu, of red starched tulle, over it an ankle-length snakeskin coat. She wears trainers, carries a small bag, on her head a kind of peaked cap. She tiptoes past the kitchen, bathroom and lavatory. She holds her breath. With her fingertips she touches the constantly flickering set of lights. She goes into the living-room, groping for the light switch on the wall. The lamp with the shade comes on and the room fills with a soft green light.* **Tanya** *pauses a moment, gazes at the walls and the ceiling, sits on the floor by the threshold, covers her face with her hands, weeps.*

Ludmila *and* **Sergei**'s *room.*

Tanya (*very softly sings*) 'Good night . . . good night . . . good night . . . good night . . .'

Ludmila *goes from the kitchen to her own room, wipes away her tears, sobs. She stops at the door, looks in surprise at* **Tanya**.

Ludmila (*loudly*) I've said it countless times, the rooms need locks! Communism! A thief's den! That idiot Vanya hands over the keys to anyone who asks. Looking for the woman of his life, he is! Or has she come for the Cyclops? You! This is not a private address, you're at the CDSR, central depot for stupid runts. He thinks he runs this place, we should dance to his tune! I've told him a hundred times: 'You are not the boss, Dima! We all are!' The door wide open! Help yourself! The lunatic asylum's next door. They take in the scarecrows from the entire neighbourhood. (*Is silent.*) Geese. (*Is silent.*) Lights. (*Is silent.*) Sergei, Ivan! (*Is silent.*) Hello!

Silence.

Tanya (*singing again*) ' . . . Good night, sleep tight, good night, goo-oo-d night, dear friends . . . (*Pause.*) Good night . . .'

Ivan *and* **Sergei** *come into the room. They say nothing. Look at* **Tanya**.

Silence.

Sergei   There's a hole in my arse! Hurrah! Hu-rrahhh!

Tanya (*softly, in tears*)   'Good night . . . good night . . .'

Ivan (*is silent*)   Hello.

Tanya   The New Year tree . . . where is it? The lamp, yes, but the tree, where?

Ludmila   Tree?

Tanya   There has to be. It's how I imagined it, I come in, there's a tree. A tree, mother, father, Aunty Lydia, Dima, Dimotshka playing his little yellow violin . . .

Silence.

Ludmila (*not moving*)   Tanyechka . . . You've grown. You've changed. You look better. (*Pause.*) I minded you, don't you remember?

Tanya   Minded me?

Ludmila   You do remember me, don't you?

Tanya   Remember?

Ludmila   Me?

Tanya   I don't think we've met . . .

Ludmila   Tanyechka . . .

Tanya   What? Why are you staring like that?

Ludmila   Tanyechka, it's all flown right out of your mind in these last ten years. You've forgotten us, forgotten your country, well, we've aged, we've changed, Ivan, Sergei, here, quick! Tatyana Danilovna has arrived! Tanyechka, our beautiful little Tanyechka, she's here!

All three throw themselves on the ground, wail, sob, embrace **Tanya**.

Tanya (*repeats*)   'Good night, good night, sleep tight . . .' All together please.

All (*sing softly in unison*)   'Good night, sleep tight . . .'

Pause.

Tanya   I always dreamed I'd come home and sing this . . . Where's mother? Where's father? Where's Aunty Lydia? Where's Dima Dimochka? Where?

Silence.

Ludmila   Aunty? Mother? Father? They're dead, Tanyechka . . .

Tanya   Dima, is Dima dead too?

Ludmila   Not yet, no! He's alive! Don't get so worked up! He'll be here in a minute. He waited. But then he left.

Tanya (*is silent, looks at* **Ludmila, Sergei, Ivan**)   Who are you? Who?

Ludmila   She's forgotten it all, all gone clean out of her mind. Emotion! It's us, Tanyechka, us, us. All together: 'Good night, good night!'

Ivan, Ludmila *and* **Sergei** *sing to* **Tanya**. *She looks at them with round eyes. Pause.*

Ludmila   We waited, Lord, did we wait! Or we'd have noticed when you came in.

Tanya   I had father's key. The golden key to my childhood . . . Here. I've always worn it round my neck and whenever I was undressing and anyone asked me: 'What's that?' – I'd say proudly: 'The key to my Moscow flat.'

Pause. **Ivan, Ludmila** *and* **Sergei** *sing:* '*Good night . . .*' *Pause.*

Ludmila   What is this, a singsong! Get into the kitchen, fetch some water! Quick, you can see how emotional she is!

Sergei *and* **Ivan** *as if at a command run to the kitchen, stumbling over the threshold.*

Tanya (*quietly, to* **Ludmila**)   Who are they?

Ludmila   Oh, Tanyechka! Have you forgotten? Forgotten! Sergei's my husband, not officially on paper, but what difference does that make? Sergei was your late father's chauffeur, may he rest in peace, such a good man! He liked to

employ simple countryfolk, and that's why we stayed on!
Sergei's still chauffeuring, he drives one of these co-operative
businessmen around, and Ivan, he was the gardener at your
dacha, lived there, only they took the dacha away when your
father died. I had nowhere to go so I popped in here, so did
Sergei, we wanted to look after your property and so we have,
right to this minute. Don't you remember, there were so many
of us? When your father died they all ran off, the ingrates!
Only we've been here ten years, keeping guard . . .

Tanya   Yes, we had a huge dacha. Just outside Moscow,
three floors . . . Stables!

Ludmila   Ah, why even talk about it? They took it
instantly, instantly! We dragged out a few things, brought
them here. Vanya, poor man, out of a job, so he retrained, he's
a projectionist now in a cinema, and I'm at a factory. Ah, but
the dacha, forget about it! Instantly, the very day your father
was killed, he died and they took it back. Those were hard
times before perestroika . . .

Tanya   Keep quiet! Don't say that!

Ludmila   What can you do, Tanyechka, of course it was
harder before perestroika, much. Easier now, what with
freedom of speech and all that . . .

Tanya   I mean stop repeating: 'Your father died, he's dead,
he was killed.' I'm not mad. I've understood. That'll do.

Ludmila   Oh, forgive me, my dear, my precious, my
Tanyechka!

Ivan *and* **Sergei** *come running with two glasses of water.*

Tanya (*drinks the water, her teeth knock against the glass*)   Dear
God, a Russian glass, I've not seen these for a hundred years
. . . a Russian glass –

Ivan   They don't have them there?

Tanya   No. Not these . . . no. (*Sobs.*) 'Good night, good
night . . .'

Ivan, Ludmila, Sergei (*in chorus, standing before* **Tanya**)
'Good night, good night . . .'

Silence.

Ludmila   Where's your . . .

Tanya   What? What did you say?

Ludmila   Your things, Tanyechka? Your luggage? Where is it? Or are you travelling light? With just a bag?

Tanya   Luggage?

Ludmila   Luggage, luggage. Hand luggage, a suitcase . . .

Tanya (*rummages in her handbag*)   My money's here, but a case . . . I think I forgot my case at the airport . . .

Ivan   You what?

Tanya   Not forgot, forgot deliberately, I didn't collect it. First of all, I was so nervous when we landed, I think I took some pills, such a long flight, we changed planes twice . . . Then at the airport the three letters surrounded me, I spotted them immediately. They were everywhere . . . The three letters are after me . . .

Ivan (*after a pause*)   What three letters?

Tanya   You know which. The usual three.

Sergei (*after a pause*)   Ah yes. The usual three. We know.

Tanya   Yes, but don't say them. The three letters are spying on me and they began right at the airport. You do understand what I'm saying? The three letters?

Pause.

Ludmila   I'm not quite with it, Tanyechka. What three letters are spying on you?

Tanya (*after a pause, whispers*)   KGB. I only just shook them off: into a taxi without my luggage and quickly away to where a tree awaits and so does my flat . . . David got out in Gorki Street, he was so ecstatic he wanted to stroll in Moscow: the snow falling, he loves it, but I couldn't wait to be home, home with the magic key tight in my fist . . .

Silence.

Ludmila   KGB? They got rid of them long ago.

Tanya   Well, that's a fairy tale! The network is still here.
(*Pause.*) Why are you looking at me like that?

Sergei   Who's David?

Tanya   My friend, we travelled together. He's strolling
down Gorki Street, it's not far and he knows the address, he'll
find me. This is so exotic for an American . . .

Silence.

Ivan   Yes, Gorki Street. Tverskaya. Peshkov Street.

Ludmila   But Tanyechka, your things, your luggage! You
forgot all of it, everything? How did you manage that?

Tanya (*gets up, walks about the room, irritated*)   Good heavens,
I've already said the three letters were following me, I had to
run. It's not important . . . My name's on the case, I expect
they'll bring it later . . .

Ludmila   They, Tanyechka? Who?

Tanya   Oh . . . the workmen, the airport staff at
Sheremyetovo . . .

Silence.

Ludmila   Yes, oh yes, they'll bring it all right. A large case,
was it?

Silence.

Sergei   Don't worry. I'll phone, I know one of the porters
. . . No: better give me the receipt. I've a bike, I'll race there
and back, I'll sort it out. Don't worry.

Tanya   You'll race there? How very kind . . .

Sergei (*holds out his hand*)   The receipt?

Tanya   Receipt? Receipt, receipt . . . I did have some little
piece of paper . . . (*Rummages in her handbag.*) I've never carried
so much cash, my bag's full of dollars . . . I was told there were
no cash machines in Moscow so I'd need to bring some . . . (*To*
Ivan, *holding out a handful of dollars.*) Hold this for me, I can't
find it . . .

She looks for the receipt in her handbag. **Ivan** *stands with arms outstretched, the dollar notes in his cupped hands, looks at them.*

Found it. This? (*Gives* **Sergei** *a piece of paper, takes the money from* **Ivan** *and stuffs it back in her handbag.*)

Sergei   Fast as a fly. There and back. No problem.

Hurries to the front door, puts on more clothes, goes.

Tanya   I've forgotten: who is he? Can he be trusted? What's his name? He's not with the three letters, is he? His eyes have that look . . .

Ludmila   Tanyechka, there are no three letters spending the night here! Sergei is my husband. And me, I was your maid, you've forgotten it all. I used to race around, tidying, dusting. No?

Tanya (*is silent*)   It's coming back. You dusted . . . Is Aunty Lydia really dead? Aunty, Dima's mother? Has she died? Are you lying?

Ludmila   Of course she's dead! She was still young, fifty-eight, ten years ago, that was. She did miss your mother and father, oh, did she miss them! No one's lying, she's dead.

Tanya (*is silent*)   You're lying. I don't know, perhaps – perhaps you're all with the KGB. Anything's possible . . .

Silence.

Ludmila (*angry*)   That's right, we're with the KGB. With the Stasi. With Mossad. All of us, we're straight from Tel Aviv. Thank you, Tanyechka! After ten years of waiting! Thank you!

She bursts into tears, turns to the wall. **Tanya** *says nothing.*

Tanya   Don't be offended! I'm sorry. My nerves are in a dreadful state, I can't think straight, I'm sorry . . .

Ludmila   I'm not offended, me, no! Have another sip from that fantastic glass. That dress in this cold, and that flimsy coat, no lining even, you need a fur. Oh, but don't you look good: sweet as a berry, forty-five and still a cherry.

Tanya   I'm thirty. It's snakeskin. Warm.

The front door opens, **Dima** *comes into the corridor. He carries a black violin case. He wears a black patch over his left eye.* **Dima** *is unshaven, slovenly, looks much older than thirty. His scarf and his sailor's jacket are also black: the buttons with anchors are bright. He comes in, stops at the door, puts the violin on the floor, sits next to the goose, strokes it, smokes a cigarette, looks at the ceiling. The goose hisses at* **Dima** *like a snake.*

Ludmila   I said it because it rhymes, I didn't mean it . . .

Tanya (*walks about the room*)   'Good night, good night . . .' This isn't my room, my room was to the left of the corridor . . .

The corridor.

Hurries into the corridor. Sees **Dima**, *in panic slowly backs away against the wall, whispers:*

They've found me . . . What do you want? They're here, they've found me!

Silence.

Ludmila   Dima, Dimochka, it's Tanyechka. Give her a kiss. Come here, come on!

Tanya   That's not . . . Dimochka?

Ludmila   It certainly is Dimochka. By the goose.

Tanya   In a KGB uniform . . . Snakes in the corner, hissing . . .

Ludmila   Here we go again, KGB. That's a sailor's jacket, Dimochka bought it in the flea market. They're very in.

Tanya (*is silent*)   Dima? Him? Dima, is it you?

Dima (*smokes, laughs*)   Seems like it. Hello. Long time, no see.

Tanya *goes to* **Dima**, *kneels, is afraid to touch* **Dima**. *They are silent.*

Tanya   What's that?

Dima (*laughs*)   A goose.

Tanya   It hisses like a snake . . . (*Is silent.*) Dimochka. The little boy from my childhood, in his white shirt, he plays the violin and I'm in a white tutu, a tiny ballerina, Thumbelina, I dance under the tree and he plays and he plays . . . What are you smoking, Dimochka? Grass?

Dima   A cigarette.

Tanya   A cigarette?

Dima   A cigarette. Want one?

Tanya   Please.

She sits down next to **Dima**. *Turns the cigarette in her hands, smells it, looks at* **Dima**.

Buy papirossi . . . buy Russian cigarettes . . . Good night, dear friends . . .

Silence.

What happened to you . . . What happened . . .

Looks at herself and **Dima** *in the mirror that stands in the corridor. The set of lights keeps flickering. Outside the window the siren, the cuckoo in the clock, the goose. Everyone silent.*

Byelomor . . . Dima's smoking Byelomor . . . Lovely Byelomor . . . Lovely Russian cigarettes . . .

Ivan (*wipes away his tears*)   God be praised! She's come! I'm happy, I'm very very happy.

Silence.

Tanya   That door . . . my room? My childhood room?

Dima   My room.

Tanya   My room! Mine! My childhood! The tree! That's where it is! In there!

She leaps up from the floor, flings open the door onto a dark room. Turns on the light, but instantly turns it off again and slams the door. Looks at **Dima**.

What happened to you . . . Everything's wrong . . . all wrong . . . give me a light . . .

Dima *doesn't move.* **Ivan** *dutifully strikes a match. All are silent a long time. The doorbell rings.*

Tanya That's David . . . it must be . . . He'll be frozen, I told him he'd be cold in what he was wearing, he's so funny . . . Dear David . . .

Again the doorbell rings. **Tanya** *doesn't move.*

I haven't the strength to let him in, I can hardly move . . . Open the door!

Ludmila *and* **Ivan** *race to the door, fling it open. On the threshold stands a transvestite: in a bright dress, a towering peroxide wig, high heels.* **Tanya** *totters over to* **David,** *flings her arms round his neck, cries out sobbing:*

Tanya David! Dear David! Look! I'm home! A new life! I'm home! We'll begin a new life! It's safe here, there are no KGB here, these are our people. This is my home, David, here there are not and there cannot be any microphones or cameras. The place is clean! David! I always dreamed of coming home to a new life! I've found it, found home! David! Dear David . . .

Sobs, sinks to the floor.

David *comes down the corridor, smiling a wide white-toothed smile, waves to* **Ludmila, Ivan, Dima:**

David He-ll-oooo . . .

Ludmila *and* **Ivan** *stand speechless, their arms at their sides.* **Dima** *sits on the floor and laughs.* **Tanya,** *by the front door, weeps.*

Darkness.

Scene Two

The corridor.

The same evening, an hour later. The doors to all the rooms are open, in all the lights are on, only **Dima**'*s room is dark. In the kitchen the window has been opened wide to air, and white mist — cold air — fills the flat.* **Ivan, Ludmila** *and* **Sergei** *in coats stand in the corridor and watch as* **Tanya,** *in a dress and barefoot, washes the floor. A suitcase* *stands on the floor in* **Ludmila** *and* **Sergei**'*s room.* **Dima** *is still sitting by the door to the flat, in shirt sleeves, stroking the goose and smoking one cigarette after another.*

Tanya (*wiping the floor, gaily*)   A new life! We'll all start a new life! I'll sleep with the goose in the corridor! I'll enjoy that, so romantic! David can move in with you, you don't mind if he sleeps on the floor in my – in your room? Do you? For some reason I can't go in, but I'd like it if David could sleep in the room where I spent my childhood! (*To* **Ludmila**.) Lift your feet please. I need to wipe here.

Ludmila   Better let me do this, Tanyechka?

Tanya   No, I have to do it myself! And you, lift your feet!

Looks at **Ivan**, **Ludmila** *and* **Sergei**.

Why are you wearing coats?

Ivan   We're cold.

Tanya   Really? I'm hot. I want to air the flat, there's a sour smell. I need to wipe here, move please . . .

Sergei *and* **Ludmila** *turn and go to their room without saying a word. They begin unpacking the case, rummaging in it.* **Ivan** *goes to his room, sits under the palm, lights a candle, holds it and mumbles something.*

Tanya (*calls after them*)   You can come back later when I've finished . . . (*Wrings out the cloth.*) Strange people . . . I can't think how they got here . . . (*Wipes the floor.*) David is so gentle, Dimochka, so wonderful, I don't know anyone else like him! We met two years ago in hospital. I wasn't well at the time, so there I was, in hospital, and we met; and have hardly been apart since. David loves Russia, the Russian soul, the idea of Russia! You see, he arrives, puts on warmer clothes and off he runs back out onto the street! Your sailor's jacket suits him!

Dima   He should have changed instead of just putting on warmer clothes. They'll kill him out there!

Tanya   Why? What do you mean?

Dima   Never mind. So, you met in a nuthouse?

Tanya   We met in hospital, I was being treated for my nerves. What more do you want to know?

Dima   What is he, a boy or girl?

Tanya   Who?

Dima   Who, who. Your David. A boy?

Tanya   David? (*Is silent.*) I don't know. Does it matter?

Dima (*laughs*)   The pistol's loaded, I'll give you a treat.

Tanya   What?

Dima   The pistol's loaded, I'll give you a treat. (*Laughs, falls silent, smokes, stares at the ceiling.*)

Tanya   I am so pleased! A new life! In Moscow, here, at home, in Russia, in my own country! We'll get married in a day or two!

Dima   What?

Tanya   I know, it's my fault. I didn't mean to stay away so long, Dimochka, and we did promise to marry when I got back. Everything got so complicated. It's not too late, we'll get married in a day or two. Tell me you love me.

Dima   Madly.

Tanya   And I love you too. And all these ten years, only you. I'm a one-man woman.

Dima   What?

Tanya   Monogamous. That means all these years only you, Dimochka. (*Wipes the floor.*) You have changed horribly, that's true. I imagined someone different, all those years, quite different. Never mind. If we can bear each other, we can love each other. A new life, Dimochka! A new life!

Dima (*laughs*)   What have I done! Wasted ten years of my life.

Tanya (*quickly*)   If only you knew, Dima, Dimochka, what I've been through there . . . (*Wipes the floor.*) When mother and father died in the crash a fog descended. To this day I'm convinced they were killed, killed because almost the next day the country was in turmoil; in the East when Muslims fight amongst themselves it can be so terrible, they're so vindictive, so bloodthirsty, so ferocious, human life means nothing to them. I'm convinced the crash was rigged, officially it was an accident, the Russians didn't want conflict with the East, the unrest had already begun, just shooting at first in the streets, we were on our way to the airport with those terrible zinc boxes, with mother and father, with their mutilated bodies, I remember the airport, filthy, stinking, a special flight, a war plane for coffins, yes, after all, father was an ambassador, a VIP ... I wanted to fly to Moscow there and then, my friend stopped me, not friend exactly, acquaintance, someone on the Embassy staff, party secretary, handsome and young, we were having an affair or we were in love, I don't know, he stopped me, said I was to stay no matter what, he loved me, I kept saying, Moscow, Moscow. He wouldn't let me. Father had brought me, officially I was an interpreter, but you know what kind of interpreter I am, so there I was without mother and father. Just two months abroad with them, couldn't have been more ignorant, and literally the day after their death the country fell apart, they shot at Nikolai's car in broad daylight and Nikolai died, Nikolai, that's my friend, Muslim devils, they killed him with their kalashnikovs, vile Russians, that's what they're known for worldwide. Kalashnikovs. So there I was, alone, quite alone in the midst of chaos, and then the embassy staff panicked: one person said to drive across the border to Russia, another said something different, everyone grabbed his gold, his clothes, his money, his possessions, and all ran off like rabbits ... Then someone else from the embassy, the deputy party chairman, he was very good to me, true, later he turned out to be a scoundrel, that's a long story, I'll tell it some other time, he helped me get a boat away from that Muslim mess to Italy. Because in the East they'd begun to slaughter each other ferociously, war, who against whom – nobody understood. The embassy staff all said from Italy we could fly home, but from Italy I flew in the opposite direction, to New York, with the deputy party chairman ...

Silence.

Dima Why not to Moscow?

Tanya I don't know. I don't know. (*Is silent, wipes the floor.*)
What was there for me in Moscow? Mother and father in the
grave, I had no profession, what could I have done? Pace from
corner to corner in this flat? What was there for me in
Moscow?

Dima I was waiting for you in Moscow. Waiting, keeping a
promise. (*Laughs.*)

Tanya Stop it. That was childish nonsense. You're
laughing yourself. I took a more serious view of things.

Silence.

There's still paint on the floor. You've not repainted since we
lived here, since I lived here . . . (*Pause.*) Listen, is she wearing
mother's dresses? The one she's got on today, was that
mother's? Wasn't it?

Dima She got the lot. Your mother had cartloads of
dresses. What were we supposed to do, throw them away?

Tanya Mother loved beautiful clothes. All a bit vulgar, I
know, but still . . . It's horrible. I see mother's dresses on her
and it turns my stomach. Can't you understand?

Dima No.

Silence.

Did you work in a brothel?

Tanya It's getting cold, I'll close the window, the place has
been aired enough . . .

Goes into the kitchen, returns, wrings out the cloth.

I feel you've grown. You're sitting and I'm standing, but
you're taller. What's it like up there? Catch me a bluebird!
That's what we used to say. Catch me a bluebird!

Dima Did you?

Tanya Why?

Dima Our women all work in brothels over there.

Tanya   That's by no means certain.

Dima   You did.

Tanya   It seems so. Yes, it seems I did. At the very
beginning, though really I don't remember how I lived, or
with whom. Where, how, with whom, on what . . . Then I had
a rich lover, then he dumped me and two months ago I
realized I was monogamous, I loved you and had to fly to
Moscow. These lights are hideous, such kitsch, I'm turning
them off.

Dima   No.

Tanya   You've become weird. I tell you I love you, but you
don't react.

Dima   Should I fall into your arms?

Tanya   I was over there, but my Moscow home was always
with me. I remembered the smallest details: this house, the
bakery on the first floor on the left, on the right the bookshop
where it smells of printer's ink and where I'd buy books when
I was a child . . .

Dima   Now it sells American gear for dollars.

Tanya   Really! That's wonderful. I'll buy you something.
What would you like?

Dima   Nothing.

Tanya (*is silent*)   What happened to you, Dima? I love you
but you're cold, you're ash. What did I do wrong? Ssssh, don't
say it, we'll talk about it tomorrow, we're too nervous today
. . . Are you sure the KGB haven't bugged the flat? A new life,
but if the place is bugged . . .

Dima   You're sick, it's a doctor you need, not a new life.

Tanya   Dima, we've been apart ten years, and I love you,
oh so much! And already you're boorish!

Dima   Poor man's theatre! Everything you say hits the
same false note.

Silence.

Tanya   What do you do?

Dima   I compose music for porn films.

Tanya   Is that a profession?

Dima   It is.

Tanya   That's wonderful.

Dima   I stand in the underground underpass and play the violin.

Tanya   I feel ghastly. What do you play? Classical?

Dima   Everything I know: all ten bars of the Oginski Polonaise. Thanks to your father who tormented a servant's child with violin lessons.

Tanya   Aunt Lydia was a member of the family, not a servant. Father wanted you to be a great violinist.

Dima   I play ten bars, repeat them three hundred times a day. People throw me money: I play the wrong notes, I've only got one eye, we've always pitied fools. I'd rather stay at home, but we ran out of things to sell, waiting for you.

Tanya   The Oginski Polonaise. It's also called 'Farewell to the Motherland.' My dream was to be a ballerina, in a white tutu and you on the violin, and I'd dance 'The Dying Swan . . .'

Dima   The Dying Whore.

Tanya   In America I kept dreaming the same dream: you and I on a stage. There's a white spot on your cheek. Toothpaste. like a child: washes in the morning but doesn't wipe his face properly. Goes the entire day without looking in a mirror. Here, let me . . .

Takes a hankerchief out of her pocket, wipes **Dima**'s *face. They are silent, look into each other's eyes.*

Have you got a girlfriend?

Dima   No.

Tanya   Do you go with women?

Dima   No.

Tanya   With men?

Dima   No.

Tanya   Why?

Dima   Why not?

Tanya   Why? With no one? You're thirty, you have to sleep with someone.

Dima   Why?

Tanya   Because. Everyone does.

Dima   Because because is why I sleep alone.

Tanya   Everyone sleeps with someone.

Dima   Let them. I'm not everyone. I'm the Cyclops, a one-eyed monster. I waited for you, I believed in the promise we made when we were children. (*Laughs*.) I waited nine years. If you'd come a year ago . . . Now I'm tired. I'll go on sleeping alone. For nine years I knew you can't sleep with someone unless you love them.

Silence.

Tanya (*gets up, goes along the corridor*)   Enough, young man! Unless you love them! Of course you can! And very nicely. But not in trousers. With trousers off, wonderfully. And stop making me feel guilty. Stop exaggerating! I love you, I'm waiting. Nobody came to meet me at the airport. Don't say anything! (*Pause*.) Forgive me, I'm sorry, I didn't wipe your face properly . . .

*Kneels again, wipes **Dima**'s face.*

Such wonderful blue eyes you had, now there's only one, dead as if it were artificial.

Dima   My mates knocked it out when they were drunk.

Tanya   That's why you won't believe me! Only one eye, can't see straight! No, not a word! We won't argue! We'll marry, Dimochka, a new life begins for us tomorrow, no more underpasses, I've nobody left in the whole wide world apart from you and David, nobody, my darling! I didn't write to you because I'd nothing to write. Why be offended? You see, I've already told you ten years of my life in just a few minutes, you wrote to me, I know, a dozen letters at the beginning, then you were silent . . .

Dima   I thought you'd died, vanished, drowned in the ocean . . .

Tanya   I got your letters, got them, I had nothing to reply, don't get excited, Dimochka please, my head's splitting! First love never fades . . . How you've changed! I've never loved anyone but you!

Dima   Never fades. (*Guffaws.*) Last year Vodopyanov brought me greetings from you.

Tanya (*not listening*)   We'll get married, yes, yes, yes . . . I'm moving the mirror . . .

Dima   Move it. I'm in charge here. Put it on the landing, if you want. I'd like to smash it, I'm sick of it.

Tanya   You mustn't break mirrors, it's unlucky! I'll see if the wall is bugged . . . A new life means we must . . .

Dima   You're sick.

Tanya *drags the mirror, it now stands in the middle of the corridor. She feels the wall, sits on the floor, takes a deep breath.*

Outside the window the siren again, the cuckoo cuckoos, the goose cries. **Tanya** *returns to the corridor, sits on the floor.*

Tanya   My head's splitting, tension, I must take something . . . We'll hang a rug on the wall. Though rugs frighten me, it's so easy to hide bugs behind them, but we'll hang one here, we'll make this my world like when I was a child. When I was a child a rug hung here behind the door, above my bed. Birds of paradise spread dark mysterious feathers, the four eyes of a strange creature blazed, in a distant meadow by a castle black children ran; later in New York I'd feel I was meeting those black children, but they were grown up now, adults, black as black and strong, so often I'd meet them: one night going home on a bus I was sitting at the back on a hard, uncomfortable plastic seat and at the front a black man got in,

tall, black, almost blue, I recognized him instantly, the little
black boy from my childhood, the one from the rug, he'd
grown up, he came along the bus and sat down next to me, the
instant he got on the bus it filled with kitchen smells, shut your
eyes and you weren't on a bus at all but in a kitchen, the small
smoky backyard kitchen of a run-down restaurant: cramped,
awkward, no room for two people to move, oil sizzling in a
pan, red meat, a green cabbage in an aluminium bowl, and all
the time the black man's sitting beside me and I smile because
he's a part of me, he's from my childhood, from the rug in my
room, there he sits, tired and with this wonderful kitchen
smell: even the earring in his ear hangs tiredly, his hands are
folded on his knees, the poor man wants to sleep, his eyes are
shut, the side of his head rests against the misted window of the
bus, and he smells wonderfully of delicious kitchen smells . . .
My headache's a little better. (*Pause.*) I used to lie on my bed,
turn to the wall and gaze at the rug, the forest, the birds of
paradise, the little black children, and dream with eyes wide
open of being there, in that forest, being a princess there so
that a one-eyed monster would love me and in the morning
when my dream was over he'd turn into a beautiful prince,
called Prince Dima . . .

Dima A one-eyed monster, yes, but turn into a prince, no,
no matter how hard I try . . .

Tanya I didn't mean to hurt you, I'm sorry. Where is my
rug?

Dima Sold.

Tanya You sold my bird of paradise?

Dima For booze. You had so many rugs. The moths were in
them. I let them sell whatever they wanted. I sold things too.
They came for a day and they stayed and this madhouse
would be boring without them. We've buried you . . .

Tanya Yes. But then, why leave well alone? These lights
are infuriating! So is that bird. It keeps screeching.

Dima I programmed it to cuckoo every fifteen minutes. I
dropped it when I was drunk . . .

Tanya   Did you sell everything? Didn't you have money for food?

Dima   For food, yes. For drink, no. (*The goose cries.*)

Tanya   Give me a cigarette . . . (*Smells the cigarette, turns it in her hands.*) Byelomor. A Byelomor . . . in New York a pack costs seven dollars. Mashed and dried chicken shit, stuffed into cardboard rolls . . . Why the goose?

Dima   At the market an old woman had him under her arm, he was screeching loud enough to wake all Moscow. I was drunk, sentimental, and felt sorry for him. The old woman said he'd perish because his mate had. If a goose dies, so does the gander. Grief. They're tender-hearted birds. He needs his throat cut. He's dying of loneliness.

Tanya   Loneliness, lonely, loveless, lifeless . . . Goosey goosey gander, whither do you wander, can't go this way, can't go that, and can't go home because the old grey wolf's in town. I need the toilet.

Takes her bag, goes to the lavatory.

Ivan *goes into the corridor, looks round scared.*

Ivan   Dima, lend me some money. Until tomorrow.

Dima   Fuck off, Ivan.

Ivan   You don't change, Dima. We're strangers here at this festival of life. Will she lend me money, do you think? Why not? The rich are supposed to help the poor.

Dima   Ask her.

Ivan   She will. I will ask. I'm not Kaltenbrunner. She will.

Goes back to his room, sits under the palm with the candle, shoots himself in the forehead with his fingers:

Bam, bam, bam, bam, bam, bam . . .

Ludmila *comes into the corridor.*

Ludmila   Where is she? What did she say?

Dima   She says, while the trams are still running and before the tarmac melts, get your fucking selves out of here . . .

Ludmila   That's not funny, Dima. Not funny at all. You've turned into a heartless swine, Dima. I've been meaning to tell you for quite some time.

Goes back to her room. With renewed energy **Ludmila** *and* **Sergei** *rummage in* **Tanya**'s *suitcase.*

The lavatory door flies open. **Tanya** *stands in the doorway. Bursts into loud laughter.*

Tanya   'Moscow, how much that word means, how it echoes in a Russian heart!' I knew what I was missing! (*Sings.*) 'Good night, good night!' I must step into my new life, my first steps. 'Land of mine, I love thee with a love forever true.' 'Lovely is life, and that's not news!' (*Laughs loudly.*) I must buy the poor gander a goose! 'No foe shall ever make thee bow thy head! Oh Moscow, golden Moscow mine, my heart lies at thy feet!' I'll build a fence and they can live here! She'll lay eggs, they'll have baby geese, goslets, gooskins, ugly ducklings that will turn into swans. The dance of the little swans. The Bolshoi! I'm trying to say that we'll buy them a little house on the outskirts, a farm, our own little goose factory! 'Hear time's pulse – BAM! far afield – BAM!' (*Laughs loudly.*) Goose and goose liver, I adore it! Not a good idea! May they live and enjoy life and swim in the gutter! 'There was an old woman and she had three jolly geese! One white, one grey, all three gay!' (*Shrieks with laughter.*) I was wrong, Dima, these are wonderful lights! They remind me of my lovely lovely childhood! When the blazing sun is gone, when he nothing shins upon, then you show your little light, twinkle, twinkle, all the night. Do you remember? I'm the best in the class! Top marks fly into my exercise books like doves! Aunt Lydia always said never carry your satchel with the clasp on the inside or you'll only get Ds. I couldn't have cared less then, now I always carry my bag with the clasp on the outside! I must buy him a goose or he'll die, I couldn't bear it, I'd die too . . .

Dima (*is silent*)   He'll die anyway. He's monogamous. He won't like your goose. He'll die.

Tanya   I'm not listening! He will like her. He's just an animal, he couldn't care less.

Dima   He's not just an animal and he does care.

Tanya   I'm buying him a goose.

Dima   Go on.

Tanya   As you like, but God is my witness, I tried to help him, there's still time, tomorrow, the day after, a new life ahead of us, Dima, so many good things! (*Cries.*) I loved you, Dima! Not you, of course, the other one, the one I invented. I thought of you so often in New York, there's a cigarette advertisement, you see it everywhere you go, a beautiful, smiling, blue-eyed you, yes, you with a cigarette in your mouth, remember what we used to say: we're puffing up our muscles. (*Laughs loudly.*) There you were on the advertisement, the spitting image! Every day our eyes met, Dimochka! I'd say to him: 'Why are we not together, you and I? Why do we tread different paths?' You were silent, smiled, smoked your cigarette! So I answered my question myself: 'We're not together, Dimochka, is that why you're smoking that muck?' (*Laughs loudly.*) I know: you can advertise Russian cigarettes! Brilliant! With one eye, cigarette in mouth, in your sailor's jacket, puffing up your muscles! (*Laughs loudly.*) Forgive me, I'm sorry, I keep thinking you're teasing and you're about to say, just like when we were children: I'm not playing any more, and you're going to take off those clothes and be the way you were in New York, the you in the cigarette advertisement, the one I . . . I invented . . .

Silence.

Dima   What did you do in the lavatory?

Tanya   What did I do? I had a pee. (*Laughs loudly.*) I took some pills. They calm me. Aspirin, they work . . . You're drinking wine. (*Takes the cup at* **Dima***'s feet, looks in it, is silent.*) I can't stand alcohol. I get drunk on life, the sun, the sky, the air, the stars! 'Life, I love you!' 'Free and proud, his native land he strides! Tender shines the dawn upon the Kremlin's walls! With daybreak the Soviet nation wakes!' (*Pause. She*

takes a deep breath, looks in the cup.) It's good to be home, so good
. . . Aunt Lydia used to give me milk in this cup, I'd drink and
see my face at the bottom, my eyes. Aunty Lydia'd say:
'Tanya, you've got gurgling eyes!' (*Laughs*.) Dear Aunt
Lydia! How I loved her . . . Do you remember how we played,
went to the circus, the zoo, don't you remember? Wasn't it
wonderful? (*Sings*.) 'Lenin is with us always! Lenin lives on in
me! In my grief, in my hope, in my joy!' (*Laughs loudly*.) When
I was little I thought there was somebody at the bottom of the
cup: somebody big and with staring eyes. (*Looks into the cup, is
silent*.) In his own world and gazing up with frightened,
watchful eyes. A reflection. Re-flec-tion. (*Pause*.) Re-
demption, re . . .

Dima   Revulsion.

Tanya   Why revulsion? This is so chaotic, I forgot to kiss
you. That suits you! But you need to wash and get your hair
cut and . . . and . . . (*Laughs loudly*.) and put in an eye! I'm
sorry, I'm stupid, I forgot. I'll do it now . . .

She kisses **Dima**, *is silent, smiles*.

I'm an idiot. Always was . . . made it all up . . . love . . . So
creative! All come undone . . . So be it, so be it . . . There's
tomorrow, always there's a tomorrow . . . A fresh start!

Pause.

I'm sorry, thinking aloud. Stream of consciousness. You
wouldn't understand, but it doesn't matter.

Dima   Vodopyanov brought me your greetings.

Tanya (*not listening*)   Your lips have a bitter taste. Like
vermouth. Like polin. Like wormwood. Dry. You're like a
child. No. Like a long limp, limp, skinny goose neck. A
drunken goose . . .

Pause.

Wormwood. Polin. Polin . . . So many Russian words are
coming back, I haven't uttered any for three hundred
years . . .

She gets up off the floor, paces the corridor, touches the chain of lights with her fingertips, laughs.

Not true. I often spoke Russian in New York. They're over there, our people. Everywhere. Like Soviet tankers colliding in the middle of a boundless ocean, that's how it is with Russians abroad: they're everywhere, everywhere. (*Laughs.*) That ghastly fear is going . . . Yes, this place is clean, no microphones . . . KGB, I ran into them everywhere. They'd ask: you, daughter of the late ambassador, you, former member of the Komsomol, what are you doing here? (*Silent.*) I once spent hours in a restaurant with one, we laughed, he told jokes, then he showed me a pack of Byelomor and said: 'Find the number fourteen on the pack'. I couldn't. Then he turned the pack and there it was; when the pack's upside down you see it: fourteen. A repulsive number, terrible. I knew it then, this comical Russian joker was from the KGB. Give me a cigarette, I want to smoke . . . (*Lights it. Is silent.*) Well now! A fresh start! First thing tomorrow morning, out you go to work, never mind where, but to work, to work! Yes, yes!

Dima   I'll run, run. First thing.

Tanya   Don't be cross. First thing. What if I opened a shop in Moscow? You could work there. And David, all of us. A hat shop! Old hats are very fashionable now. We'll think up a good line: 'I want to be beautiful Vanya? Then be it! Manya!' (*Laughs loudly.*) We'll have men's hats, and women's, those like mushrooms, and like Marilyn Monroe wore. They'll sell like hot cakes because my shop will be in the very centre of Moscow . . .

Dima   By Lenin's tomb . . .

Tanya   You could buy it for dollars! We'll have a huge clientele, everyone will praise us, as the company's president I'll be on television, I'll give interviews on the radio, and then, then, they'll put me forward for president of Russia . . .

The siren outside the window, the cuckoo, the goose. Silence.

I loved you, all these years loved you . . . Why have you got so seedy, so washed out, so ruined, so old so quickly, why, why? (*Quickly.*) Oh God! I forgot! I haven't handed out anything yet. No presents. Russians, and we are Russians, hand out presents when they meet . . .

Dima   You hand out alms. You give presents. There's no need. I'm fine.

Tanya   Wait, don't refuse, wait, you don't know what it is! Wait!

She runs into **Ludmila** *and* **Sergei**'s *room.*

My case, is it here? I'm sorry, I didn't realise, I feel so at home . . .

Ludmila *and* **Sergei** *leap up and away from the case.*

Ludmila   We were helping you unpack, Tanyechka . . .

Tanya   Yes, yes of course, thank you . . .

She takes the case by the handle, drags it into the corridor. Rummages in the case, throwing out some glittering clothes. **Ludmila** *and* **Sergei** *come into the corridor and stare into the case.* **Ivan** *also shows up, his eyes fixed on* **Tanya**.

Tanya   Here. Found it. For you. Almost real . . .

She holds out to **Dima** *an artificial rose set in a water-filled glass.*

Dima   I don't need it.

Tanya   Give it to your girlfriend.

Dima   I don't have a girlfriend. I've told you already.

Tanya   Boyfriend.

Dima   Nor boyfriend. There's no one in my life to whom I give gifts.

Tanya   Don't hurt me. It cost nothing, it's kitsch, pretty though. I bought it on Fourteenth Street, the shops there are full of all kinds of nonsense . . .

Ludmila   Yes, we know – Shit in bulk.

Tanya   Take it, please!

Dima *holds out his hand, looks at the rose. Hides his hand behind his back.*

Dima   You bought it for me?

Tanya   I've told you, I thought about you all the time! For you!

Dima   Thank you.

He takes the rose, lets it drop, it breaks.

Ivan   You limbless scarecrow! That cost money!

Sergei, **Ludmila**, **Ivan** *and* **Tanya** *throw themselves onto the floor, pick the rose out from the pieces, pass it to each other.*

Tanya   A pity . . . So pretty . . . It flew across the ocean without breaking, wear it in your buttonhole and think of me . . .

Dima (*quietly*)   I'm sorry. I'm clumsy . . .

Tanya *throws herself on* **Dima**, *passionately kisses him, shakes him, whispers:*

Tanya   No, no, no! Dimochka! It's all right! Don't be upset! Please! Dear Dimochka, oh, I loved you! Love you! So much! I've another present for you. A toy! A little jar, with water and snow inside! If you shake it, the snow whirls round the Statue of Liberty. Wait, Dimochka!

She rummages in the suitcase.

Where is it?

Ludmila   Sergei put your Liberty in our room, on the chest of drawers. So we could all see. Sergei, fetch Liberty! Go on, quick!

Sergei *runs to his room.*

Ludmila   Careful, I'll sweep all this up before someone cuts themselves . . .

She runs to the kitchen, brings back a broom, sweeps the pieces into a pan.

Sergei *brings the toy, gives it to* **Tanya**. **Tanya** *vigorously shakes the toy, holds out her hand and puts it in* **Dima**'s hand. *They are silent.* **Dima** *shakes the toy, looks at it, holding it close to his eye. He gives a* *dry, hollow laugh, wipes away his tears.* **Tanya** *too. The goose gives a cry.*

Ludmila   We were helping you unpack, Tanyechka, I wouldn't want you to think . . . Because I for one am very glad you've come! I can talk to you about my problems, as a woman you'll understand. Being intimate doesn't come easy to me, I don't have a woman friend. He chases after women. Hardly an evening when I don't have to put on some disguise and spy on him. We've got plenty to tell each other.

Sergei   Three roublesworth. Watch it!

Ludmila   I spy on him, Tanyechka. I'll catch him yet. He chases after other women. He wouldn't if we had a marriage certificate. Only as to all intents and purposes we don't have a legal address, we can't get a marriage certificate. There's a little dress in your suitcase, honestly, it's too big for you, so is your coat. I'll find you something military instead, those horrible Soviet uniforms, they're very in right now, very . . .

Tanya   Take them, take it all, I don't want them, they're yours . . .

She hands things to **Ivan**, **Sergei**, **Ludmila**.

They only remind me of the past, we're starting a new life, this goes in the bin . . .

Ludmila   In the bin, that's right, Tanyechka, just give them to me, I've been through those already.

Tanya   Just one thing, please! You've changed twice already this evening, you keep putting on mother's dresses! Please, I implore you!

Ludmila   Dresses, which?

Tanya   That one, the green . . . Mother's dress!

Ludmila   You mother's? What has got into you, Tanyechka! Would I wear a dead person's clothes? It's mine, this dress, I bought it before perestroika, it's old, what has got into you?

Ivan   Have you got any men's clothes?

Tanya   Take it all, but leave the case, I'll sleep in it. Where's the lovely chest of Aunty Lydia's that used to stand in the corridor?

Sergei   The truth? Sold. Flea market.

Ludmila   What chest, Tanyechka? You go away for a week, stay away ten years, then turn up without a word of thanks, you're not one bit interested in us, we had nothing to eat, we waited, we looked after this flat for you, looked after your property, now you show up and want everything to be just as it was, we had nothing to eat, but you, no gratitude, no, all you do is you ask about your nurse's chest . . .

She bursts into tears. Carries the things into her room, dragging the sleeve of a dress behind her in the corridor. **Sergei** *follows her.* **Ivan** *carries some of the things into his room. They slam the doors. Pause.*

The siren wails, a strained, frightened sound, the cuckoo comes out, croaks something, the goose cries once.

Tanya (*calls after them*)   Why so offended, what have I done?

Dima (*shakes the toy, looks at it*)   She's not offended.

Tanya   They used to be so polite. They've changed: they're impertinent and nasty . . . Do you think she'll report me to the KGB? Will she?

Dima   Report you? No.

Tanya (*gets into the case, curls up*)   We used to play hide-and-seek, the chest stood here, I'd crawl in . . . I'm so frightened, Dimochka, I've dreamed for so many years of this door, now it's in front of me and I'm frightened, everything, everything's changed, this door should lead to my world . . . My streets were here, my faraway countries, my toys, my friends, my family, someone came, broke down the door, turned my world on its head, I can never, never put it right again, everything will have to be rebuilt now, rebuilt . . . Through there is the kingdom of the dead.

Dima   I didn't break down your door. I lived here. This was also my world. And still is. Come. If this is how it's to be, I've something for you too. To remember me by. For the new life, yours. Come.

He gets up, pushes the door open with his foot, goes into the room, turns on the light. **Dima***'s room is lit by a blue bulb.* **Dima** *stands at the window, looks beyond the balcony out at the city.* **Tanya** *follows him in, walks about the room, touches the walls.*

Silence.

Ludmila *and* **Sergei***'s room.*

Ludmila (*holds first one dress, then another to herself*)   So this is how capitalism is going under! Did you hear her: mother's dresses, mother's dresses! I didn't have a rag to cover my arse. Hands out old clothes! She could have brought us something new.

Sergei   A fresh turd. That David, is he a boy or a girl? (*Guffaws.*)

Ludmila   What's it to you?

Sergei   He struts like a gangster. I'm telling my boss this tomorrow, he'll piss himself.

Ludmila   He's a boy and a girl. A special slit and a carrot. That's the West. For dollars you get a slit and a plastic carrot. I could do with that.

Sergei   What for?

Ludmila   To drive you mad, you reptile. How does this look?

Sergei   Shitty. Nothing special.

Ludmila   What about this?

Sergei (*guffaws*)   Now we're talking.

They laugh loudly, put hands to their mouths, sink to the floor.

Ivan *sits in his room, spreads the clothes out on the floor, mutters to himself.*

Dima*'s room.*

Tanya   You even hear him in here.

Dima   Who?

Tanya   The cuckoo. Sweet, I'd like to throw a stone at him so he doesn't come out any more . . . Dima!

Dima (*turns round, looks at* **Tanya**)   What?

Tanya (*is silent*)   Dimochka . . .

Dima   What?

Tanya (*is silent*)   Dimochka . . . What's that in the sky?

Dima   A star.

Tanya   And there?

Dima   Another one.

Tanya   And that?

Dima   Another star.

They are silent.

Tanya   Tomorrow to the cemetery. Early. Will you show me their graves? Do you know where?

Dima   What?

Tanya   Their graves?

Dima   Yes. Your name's on the stone. I buried you a year ago.

Tanya   Thank you.

Dima   Don't mention it. There's your present, there, in the corner.

Tanya   What? Paper? Burn it . . . What is it?

Tanya *goes to the pile of paper, kneels, goes through it.*

Dima   I'm sorry. It was stupid of me to hope. How I hated your fat mother, your obtuse brainless father, how ashamed I was of my mother who toadied and slaved for them. And how I loved you. For a year, for two, for three, four, every day, every minute, you only you, you filled my world, always more wonderful, I talked to you, I wrote you letters without knowing where to send them, nine years, nine years for a plastic doll . . . A mutual friend, an old classmate of ours returned from over there a year ago, Vodopyanov, Shurik, said you'd said to say hello, and merrily bragged . . .

Tanya (*quickly*)   Vodopyanov, Vodopyanov, yes, I remember, the swine, he came to New York to sell matryoshka dolls and buy bargain-basement shit, I didn't stoop to talk to him, I'm certain he's with the KGB . . .

Dima   . . . and merrily bragged he'd slept with you and anyone who wanted could, because you, you were one of the attractions of New York's Russian emigrés: the daughter of a former ambassador of the Soviet Union, who's become a filthy whore . . .

Tanya (*laughs loudly*)   Ah, Vodopyanov, Vodopyanov . . . Lies! Lies!

Dima   Ten years of my life, ten years . . .

Tanya   The furniture needs rearranging. What made me think I'd sleep in the corridor? One of you can sleep in the corridor? I'm the mistress here. I'm sleeping here! Here! Here!

Ivan *bursts into the room, falls on his knees.*

Ivan   Tatyana Davidovna, the time has come! In God's name, I implore you! Kind friend! I beg you, give! Give to me! We're strangers here at this festival of life!

Tanya   What . . . what do you want? What is this?

Dima (*sits by the balcony*)   The traditional Russian whine!

Ivan   Silence! You don't frighten me! For ten years you tyrannized us. Like an executioner. He seized power in this flat, Tatyana Davidovna! He tyrannized! He did as he pleased! You're the mistress here and I want to ask you: Tatyana Davidovna, lend me money. You're rich. Look at the dress you're wearing. Like a foreign film star. Help poor Vanya! Take pity on poor Vanya!

Dima   Arise, oh prophet . . .

Ivan   Silence! Not a word! You don't run this place. Tatyana Davidovna, help me, help me, give!

Tanya Enough, get up, here, take what you need, take it all . . .

She takes her handbag, throws money from it onto the floor. **Ivan** *gathers it up, crawls from the room to the corridor, laughing.*

Ivan She gave, she gave . . . I'm a lucky man, a lucky man . . . I knew it . . . A big thank you, Tatyana Davidovna, I've already found a woman, she's said she'll live with me if I get money to buy a flat, you're a real human being . . .

He crawls into his room, turns out the light, sits underneath the palm, trembles, crosses himself, 'shoots' himself in the forehead:

Bam, bam, bam, bam, bam, bam . . .

Silence.

Dima That's how it is, they don't sleep together, but somehow they have children.

Tanya What?

Dima Ah well, I'm sorry. Now I'm drunk. I'm sorry. I'm past caring!

Tanya No one has ever gone down on their knees to me before.

Dima How much did you give him?

Tanya I don't know. I had two or three thousand.

Dima Roubles?

Tanya Dollars, naturally. So? He said he needed it. So? He'll start a new life.

Dima No he won't.

Tanya Why not? He said he had a woman . . .

Dima He'll put the money in a tin and bury it under the palm tree in his room. That's what he always does. At night he counts it.

Tanya Why?

Dima So he worries less, why else. Saves, Vanya does. Why did you give him money? It was stupid.

Tanya He frightened me. He's like the crazy man in the hospital. He'd always ask for a cigarette. He'd found out I was Russian, he'd keep asking me, and dribbling saliva, he had eyes, such eyes . . . 'Papirossi' he'd say, 'papirossi', as if he wanted a million and if I didn't give them, he'd die . . . (*Is silent.*) I forgot, I want to buy a goose. I haven't a cent. (*Goes down the corridor, knocks on* **Ivan**'s *door.*) Hello, hello there! I've changed my mind.

Ivan (*opens the door, looks out from the darkness, candle in hand*) What? Huh?

Tanya Give me back some dollars. I need to buy a goose . . .

Ivan Dollars? Goose? Is this a circus? A zoo? This is the Soviet Union. There are no dollars here! I know nothing.

He slams the door shut. **Tanya** *slowly goes into* **Dima**'s *room. They are silent.*

Dima He goes to work in the morning, I'll dig up the money for you then. There are no locks on doors here, I'm the boss, I didn't allow it. You'll get it back tomorrow . . .

Tanya Our palm has grown. It was a tiny little thing . . .

Dima He sits under it with a candle and thinks he's in America.

Tanya In America nobody sits with candles under palm trees. Leave him. We'll earn some more. I'm not utterly hopeless, you know. We'll earn some. And David's sure to have some. My headache's back . . . We'll borrow for the hat shop from friends in New York, I'll phone right now, no, tomorrow, they'll advertise and raise money . . .

Dima Please.

Tanya (*shouts*) I know they'll raise money, they'll try for something like this, it's a fantastic project, David should be here any minute, I'll talk to him, oh, David, where is my David, where is my saviour, so beautiful, so sweet, so easy to be with, the one person I'm close to on this earth, I love him, he's mine, for some reason I keep hoping he'll soon forget English and start speaking Russian . . .

Dima   Please.

Tanya (*still louder*)   Yes, it will happen, yes, one lovely moment when he starts speaking Russian, that heap of paper frightens me, it's not possible, it was just a joke with us, you're mad, you're from the KGB, I'm frightened, I'm burning it, I can't bear to see it, it tells me there are microphones here, I'm sure David thinks in Russian, sometimes I can even see Russian words, Russian thoughts, Russian questions, Russian answers creeping into his head, he loves Russia, my country, the Russian people, he loves them . . .

The siren, the goose, the cuckoo. A long ring at the door. **Tanya** *rushes into the corridor, opens the front door.*

David *stands in the doorway: his face covered in blood, his wig in his hands, his dress in rags, a sleeve of the sailor's jacket torn off.*

Tanya (*shrieks*)   David! What happened? They beat you? In the street? Why? Barbarians! Swine! They hit my sweet boy! What happened, David? Why?

Ludmila, **Sergei**, **Ivan** *run out of their rooms into the corridor. Raging,* **David** *smashes the mirror in the middle of the corridor, the pieces fly in all directions.* **Ludmila** *shrieks. Like a tiger,* **David** *paces up and down the corridor, his fists clenched:*

David   Fuck you, Russia! Fuck you, Russia! Fuck you, Russia! Fuck you, Russia!

All stand, motionless. In his room **Dima** *weeps.*

Darkness.

Act Two

Scene Three

Dima's *room.*

A week has passed. The flat as before. Evening.

Nothing has changed. The mirror stands where it stood — in the middle of the corridor — covered with a black cloth. The goose sits by the door. **Tanya** *is in the lavatory, singing.*

Ludmila *enters the corridor from the stairway. Takes off her coat, hangs it on the coat stand.* **Ludmila** *is in a new dress — lurex. She opens the door to* **Dima**'s *room without knocking.* **Dima** *is washing the floor.*

Dima   What?

Ludmila   Nothing. Where is she?

Dima   Here. Where have you been?

Ludmila   Where have I been? Where do you think? Chasing after Sergei. We're packing her off today to a lunatic asylum. She's mad. I'm phoning the hospital. As for her friend: a prostitute if ever there was one, escaped like her from an American lunatic asylum. I've got her KGB, KGB, ringing in my ears. Last night I dreamed my Sergei was working for the KGB. She'll take us round the bend with her. You're the boss. You phone. Let them come for her, party whore. Why's she forever on the toilet? Diarrhoea? Constipation?

Dima   Get out.

Ludmila   Shithead's found himself a job, has he? Protects her. Washes the floor! You don't frighten me. Eugh! One eye on us, the other on the ceiling! Were they that good to us you have to defend them? They sneered, tormented, we slaved for them, for the entire family . . . And now look at you!

Dima   What do you want? What?

Ludmila Sleep and forget, that's what! Her and her pederast David have wrecked my nerves all week. They stuff themselves, I've run out of everything. Three thousand roubles gone up in smoke already, I'm feeding them. I need this like the Red Army needs sore feet. What did they bring us? Nothing. A rose in a glass for three roubles, which she broke, and that was for you, not me! I'm not a convict, I don't need to cringe and smile. We don't have slaves now! We've had perestroika! Us cooks should be running the state!

Dima Cook, get into the kitchen and cook slops for Fatso!

Ludmila I asked you a question: what's she doing on the toilet? Is she boozing? Has she hidden a bottle in the tank? Has she got hashish in there? Marihuana? What's she up to?

David *in tail-coat and bow-tie comes down the corridor — he has been in the kitchen.* **David**'s *hair is smoothed straight back, as if pomaded,* **Ludmila** *shrieks.*

Ludmila God Almighty! An apparition!

David Drastueetye. Pilyad, ni pilyad, nye kiyu askaripilyat.

Ludmila Strastvui, strastvui, xher mordasti. Nu, vot shto eto po kvartirye blondayetsa? Maskarad, bardak. Got it? Like hell he has!

David Da, da.

Ludmila Trolls around the flat all day, what is he, male or female, the shitheap. I can't take it. On vorovkovati, dumayu. He's after my jewellery.

David (*pats* **Dima** *on the cheek*) Da ... da da da ...

Ludmila Svolota golubaya! They're missing you back at the madhouse. Po tebye durdom plachet. Understand my Russian?

David Kharasho, karasho.

Ludmila Kharasho. He understands bugger all! And that's all any of you in the West ever will understand about my exhausted soul, and about us Russians. Rosha kastrata.

Castrated arsehole! You and your putrid West! Doma sidish?
Our lads gave you a hiding, did they? Daren't go out? To-to.
Tut tebye nye Amerika. He sleeps in your room, does he leave
you alone at night?

David *sits down by the goose.* **Tanya** *comes out of the lavatory,*
listens.

Dima (*washing the floor*)   Go away.

Ludmila   Good thing if he did pester you. You'd get a look
inside his trousers. You could tell us what he's got. We'd learn
something. He shaves, I've seen. I'd be very interested to
know what's in his trousers. He's been done. Castrated. His
mother and father snipped them off. That pale face is typical.

Tanya   There are words in the West that Russian lacks.
Tolerance, toleration of a person's nature. Your mentality,
the mentality of Russians, is that of mental defectives. You are
intolerant. You're swine. It's wrong to say scurrilous things to
a person's face when he doesn't understand a word of Russian.
You're intolerant, you Russians! Go and milk goats! Feed
pigs! Clear off back to your villages if you don't know what
tolerance is!

Ludmila (*goes to her room, in the doorway*)   And one other
thing: turn the light off in the toilet. We pay for electricity in
roubles here, not dollars, and for us roubles is money. Roubles
may not be money to some, but we are proud of our great
country, and we are proud that our money is roubles! Lights
go off, finger on the switch and press, there are no servants
here!

Tanya   You're wearing mother's dresses again! How many
did you steal?

Ludmila   Who do you think you are! Got a residence
permit, have you? I have. Temporary, but permanent soon.
You're nobody! Prove it's your flat! I'm handing you over to a
mental hospital. You're not all there. You arrive, shit dolled
up in fancy dress, America, America! I'll see your America
fucked in the dog position. I shit on your America! The finest

people on earth are the Russians, not the Americans! Drive me out of here! Suck it!

Tanya Belt up! Servant! Silence! How dare you talk like that to your mistress!

Ludmila Shit on a mistress like you!

Tanya Fool!

Ludmila You're the fool!

Tanya Slut!

Ludmila The slut is you!

They shriek. Rush at each other, come to blows. **Dima** *sits by the balcony in his room, makes no move.* **David** *sits by the door, strokes the goose, makes no move. The cuckoo cuckoos, outside the window the siren wails.*

The fight ends. **Ludmila** *goes crying to her room.* **Tanya** *sits sobbing on the floor in the corridor.*

Tanya Shameless . . . They never crossed the threshold before, neither seen, nor heard, nobody even knew their names, now they're insolent, they're the masters now . . . Once upon a time there was a hare that lived in a straw hut, and a fox in a hut of ice, and then it was spring and the ice began to melt, so the fox moved in with the hare, made himself at home and chased away the hare. This was our world, a clean, quite, affluent home, peaceful, Moscow hospitality, intelligent people lived here, now's it's a hostel, a thieves's den: we had everything, property, money, respect, now I'm out on the street, I've nothing, no one needs me, my world has been trampled upon and destroyed . . .

Goes into **Dima**'s *room.*

Can't you protect me? Is this the man I loved! This animal I thought about for ten years!

Dima She's right. You should turn out the toilet light.

Tanya Thank you. Thank you, Dima.

Dima Time you got used to it. You've fought with her seven times this week.

Tanya   Thank you for counting. That's Russian hospitality for you. Look at David! I'm ashamed for you. The poor boy's terrified, beaten up, tormented, persecuted, destroyed! He sleeps and dreams of America!

Dima   Let him go back. No one's keeping him.

Tanya   We haven't a cent. You've taken the lot. I showered the servants with presents. I gave away all my money.

Dima   You manage to find money for other things.

Tanya   Implying what? Besides, that's my business and David's! This country is barbaric, you've a different mentality, we do it to tone up, nothing wrong with that! And I'm not leaving! I've come to build a new life and I'm going to build a new life! Otherwise you'll say I was defeated, conquered by your vulgar banality! You waited for me! You waited for a call to America, for me to invite you so you could come and buy cheap clothes! I know you Russians! Waited!

Silence. **Dima** *sits by the balcony, gazes at the ceiling.*

She goes into the corridor, sits down by **David**, *rests her head on his knees.*

A wild animal . . . bores into you with his one eye . . . A monster, Cyclops . . . (*Whispers.*) David, look, microphones in the ceiling. KGB. They listen all the time, and these people here all work for the KGB, they'd like me to snap. You see: the phone hasn't rung all week, not once! In the past the phone never stopped ringing, thousands of people, friends, they phoned, now – the phone's silent! Because the phones are bugged, they're listening in, they want to be rid of me, make me vanish, kill me, crush me, trample me! I won't let them!

Grabs the phone, throws it to the floor, stamps on it. The siren outside, the cuckoo.

Microphones, there, look! There! And cameras! You won't get me!

Tears the clock from the wall, it lies there, she stamps on it.

In her room **Ludmila** *lies on her bed crying.* **Dima** *in his room doesn't make a move.* **David** *strokes the goose, smiles.* **Tanya** *grabs her handbag, flings open the lavatory door, locks herself in. Sobs.*

David Crazy ... crazy ... crazy ... (*Sings softly.*) Ay yuchnem, ay yuchnem ... yeshcho raz, yeshcho raz ... ay yuchnem ...

David *takes a fragment of mirror that stands by the door, looks at himself, touches the bruise under his eye, wiggles his eyebrows. The lavatory door opens.* **Tanya** *goes swaying, smiling up to* **David**.

Tanya Not broken mirrors, David. Unlucky ... (*Sits on the floor, rests her head against* **David**'s *knee.*) David, there's no snow in Moscow. I'd have gone out, I can't get past the entrance. Everything's changed. Ambassadors' children, Central Committee secretaries lived in this building, it was clean, we had a porter, now, disgusting, vomit everywhere, dogs by the unlit entrance, old women with sacks on their backs, obscenities on the walls, the staircase, the cooks have taken over ...

David *strokes* **Tanya**'s *head, smiles.*

David Crazy ... crazy ... crazy ...

Tanya (*lies there, smiling*) You've kind hands, David ... Aunt Lydia'd count the knuckles on her hand if she forgot what month it was. January, February, March, April ... the valleys, the months with thirty days, the hills, the months with thirty-one ... Isn't that amusing! David, beautiful hands are important. The hands and eyes are the person. There are coarse hands with short, stubby, ingrown nails; bite and chew your nails, yours are a strangler's hands with hair on the joints, dark thin hair or blonde, or even more repulsive, red; and it grows from little black spots like blackheads, then at the wrist more hair, black and thin, I've so often met those hands, they're coarse, they squeeze, pummel, they don't know how to caress, to touch, to be gentle. Almost everyone has hands like that ... three times I met hands that were different; yours, Nikolai's, and one other person. Hands with long, long, slender fingers that droop, washing in water, rosy

water running over them: rosy hands, rosy nails and palms
with long deep lines and nails that have tiny white spots . . .
(*Laughs softly.*) Do you know what a white spot on your nail
means? Aunt Lydia told me it means something new, a
present, success, happiness, if you cut off the white spot with
scissors, then fate brings you your present that very day . . .
I've not had white spots for years . . . I told that to an
American, he laughed and said, if there are white spots on
your nails it means your body lacks magnesium . . . Stupid
American, he had stumpy peasant's hands . . .

David (*smiles, strokes* **Tanya**'s *head*)   Crazy . . . crazy . . .

Tanya   If a person's hands don't interest me, that person
doesn't . . . But when I saw his hands, his eyes, then I could
think of no one but him. He gave me his photograph, I held it
up and the photograph began to fade, the face vanished, sank
into oblivion and I woke and I couldn't remember his face,
only his hands, his kind gentle hands, I can see them now . . . I
like to look at the hands of strangers. If his hands attract me,
he can scowl, be unfriendly, angry, there's something about
him. I look at hands on buses, in restaurants, on the street, and
I wonder what this man or that boy did with those hands: held
a glass of wine, his little finger raised, the higher the finger, the
more remote the province he's from! – Oh, those country
boys, I know so many! – Hands washing hair, holding a comb,
he looks at himself in the mirror, a pimple on his forehead! A
sweet pimple! He's furious because of this pimple on his
forehead, he feels it with his finger, then slicks back his hair,
dials a number, holds the receiver, talks to someone, opens the
door, goes down the street, hands in the pockets of his old
jeans, then those hands take off his clothes, he lies down on a
bed with someone he loves, he embraces, strokes a body, the
body of the one he loves, a delicious body . . .

Dima *comes into the corridor, sits in the doorway. Looks at* **Tanya**.

Dima   You still haven't gone to the cemetery.

Tanya   Killjoy, idiot . . . I still haven't been to the cemetery.
I've told you, I can't go on the underground. I don't have a
car. The servants are too well off, our former chauffeur refuses

to take me, his mistress, to the cemetery! And what's there to see? My own name on a gravestone? Thank you! Buried! I've no money for a taxi, my former gardener has my money! The servants have become insolent.

Dima   I'll dig up your money right now.

Tanya   Don't you dare take the last crust from a beggar! I don't need anything!

Dima   I'll give you fifty kopecks for the underground.

Tanya   I can't travel on the underground.

Dima   Millions do every day.

Tanya   I'm not millions! I'm an individual! I'm the centre of the universe! I'm delicate! A delicate thing! I'm a delicate sensitive creature, I'm – a goose! Even in America I didn't travel on the underground! Those escalators drone and I feel I'm descending from heaven into the underworld, into a hell where bones crackle like matches, like twigs, the escalators roll and roll and they tear at my skin, my eardrums! Tell him I can't bear it, David, the trains, the windows, the rails, the tiles, the stink, I'd die instantly . . . And Dimochka, they're down there, everywhere, the three letters, the KGB with cameras . . .

David   KGB, KGB . . .

Tanya   They sit in big white rooms and watch us, they examine us under a microscope as if we were flies, worms, insects, and I don't want to be an experimental insect! I cannot travel on the underground!

Dima   Tanya . . . Listen please, Tanya . . . You're ill . . .

Tanya   But you're well! Brainless scarecrow! You've cables, not nerves! What do you know of my delicate soul, my response to the world! Don't dare tell me I'm ill, don't dare, you putrifying corpse! You polluted my world, mine, my childhood was here, now there's only death, that heap of paper, this tiny space was all I had on this earth, a few square metres of childhood, you crawled in and trampled them with your boots! You'd put me in an asylum, you've already phoned, a car's on the way! They won't take me alive, I'll take an overdose or cut my throat! It takes a fool like me to put up with your world! With you, with that feeble-minded Ludmila, with her cretinous husband, with that idiot with his palm, I'll throw the lot of you out, sleep in the underground, you travel on it, your nerves can take it! I'll hand you over to the KGB, I'll sell this flat to a Chinese, a Vietnamese, an American, a German, I don't care who . . . You'll be gone!

Shakes **David** *by the shoulders, pulls him up.* **David** *chuckles.*

David! My dear little boy! You're a man, be blunt and firm with this pack of reptiles, tell them: 'Get out, swine, you don't belong here!' Get out! Get out!

Dima *seizes* **Tanya**'*s hand, drags her into his room, pushes her to the floor.*

Silence.

David, help me . . . There are hands, David, everywhere, through the wall, touching me . . . everywhere hands . . .

Dima   Ssssh . . . sssh. Calm down. It's all right.

Tanya   David? Is it you?

Dima   It's me.

Tanya   So dark. I'm frightened.

Dima   What's there to be afraid of?

Tanya   Give me your hand . . . I like it here . . . So quiet, peaceful . . . I have you, David, that's good . . . You're speaking Russian, David . . . I knew you would . . . My only saviour, David, you . . . I hold your hands and feel calm . . .

Dima   Ssssh . . . Quiet . . . Calm down . . . I'm here . . . I've decided: we will get married . . . I'll make you well, I can . . . I'm grateful . . . You gave me years of calm, of love, what if it did all happen only in my head, in my world, in this room. I love you. We'll make a fresh start, it's not too late, there's still time, my dearest, my darling, it's not too late . . .

Tanya *lights a lighter, looks* **Dima** *in the face.*

Tanya   Who are you?

Dima I'm Dima, your Dima . . .

Tanya You're trying to rape me . . . Your hands are
shaking with excitement, I can feel . . . You invented a
beautiful girl, for ten years wrote her letters, now you blame
me for not being that person . . . Don't touch me . . .
Everywhere hands . . . all over me, hands . . .

*She crawls along the floor into a corner. Again lights the lighter. Looks at
the pile of paper. Is silent.*

This paper, why is it in my world? . . . I'm burning it . . . You
tried to rape me . . . (*Lights the papers.*) I know you tried to rape
me! You're all the same! Help! Fire! We're on fire! Fire! Help!

Leaps up from the floor, runs into the corridor, throws herself at **David**,
clings to him. **Dima** *jumps up, stamps, beats with his jacket, puts out
the flames.*

Fire! We're on fire! Help! We're on fire! We're on fire! . . .

David (*smiles, strokes* **Tanya**'*s head*) Crazy . . . crazy . . .

The lines of small writing on the pages curl in the fire.

Darkness.

Scene Four

The kitchen.

The next day, evening.

*It is dark in the flat, only in the kitchen a red bulb on the ceiling is lit. At
the table, hair done, calm, tidied up and clean, sit* **Ludmila**, **Tanya**,
Sergei, **Dima**, **David**. *They are eating soup. The lights in the
corridor have gone. So has the cuckoo, and the goose. The sirens outside
as before wail intermittently in anguish. In the flat all are quiet and in a
state of shock.*

Ludmila (*eating soup*) No, of course, Tanya, I'm thrilled
when people speak foreign instead of Russian, only they
should do it in trousers, Tanya, in trousers. So, David, you're
always welcome, only in trousers next time, because our
Russian mentality isn't in favour of toleration and doing what

comes naturally. I'm smoking too much, it's the excitement
because you're leaving, I'm getting nicotine poisoning. You
will come back, won't you? We'll look after your flat. It would
be nice to see you again. (*Eats and smokes.*)

Sergei (*hiccups*)   Who's thinking of me then?

Ludmila   It's raining. Nature herself is weeping, Tanya,
because you're leaving us. Eat up, eat for the journey.

Tanya   I'm sorry, I feel rather ill, I must do something
about my nerves. It feels good here, so quiet, so good here at
home in my own country. A quiet corner at the heart of
Russia. No wars, no killings. Home. Peaceful and cosy. In
America I shall remember that my world is here, quiet and
snug, I'll come back when I need to run away from them
there, from the noise and the violence. Being with you will
calm my nerves. Lyudochka, I've been meaning to ask,
what's that on your wall?

Ludmila   It's a tradition with us, with Sergei and me. We
stick labels from bottles on the wall.

Tanya   How sweet. The kitchen will soon be covered with
them from floor to ceiling.

Ludmila   We're not alcoholics, except on holidays. It's
redecorating really. It's practical and looks nice. When we
have guests we like to say: 'Here's what we knocked back,
Sergei and me.' Eat up, eat . . .

Tanya   David, we Russians love birthdays. Birthdays and
New Year are the best times of the year. In three hundred
years people will celebrate nothing but birthdays and the
New Year and they'll always be happy. Yes, yes, yes. At first
people will still be angry, for a long time still fight wars, then
they'll calm down, a great love will descend upon the earth
and everyone will be happy. I believe that. All Russia will be a
garden, an orchard, apples and cherries. And Russians
everywhere will come back home, back to their own country,
because that's where life is best and where the finest people
live, in Russia. David, for you Christmas is important, for us,
the New Year and birthdays. Happy birthday, Dima. How

quiet it is. In a moment the door will open and mother come in: 'How are you, Mother? Mother, I do love your blue dress, it suits you so . . . Is father at work? Ah well . . .'

Ludmila   You'd think it would get on her nerves going on about those dresses.

Tanya   What?

Ludmila   Eat before your journey.

Tanya   Something's missing, I can't decide what.

Ludmila   The cuckoo.

Tanya   Ah, yes. Dima, I meant to tell you, I knew aunty died the very day she did. It was in the winter, at night, suddenly a ladybird flew into my flat, I had a dirty, shabby little room on the third floor. I was shutting the window, in New York there are sirens from dawn to dusk like in Moscow, and suddenly, a ladybird. It settled on my hand. Its little wings trembled. I knew instantly: Aunt Lydia has died and her soul has flown to me to say goodbye. I felt claustrophobic with her huge soul in that little room, I opened the window, put the ladybird out and said: 'Forgive me, Aunt Lydia, forgive me . . .' And lay down and cried . . .

Ludmila   Eat up, eat.

Sergei (*hiccups*)   Who is it keeps thinking of me then?

Tanya   David, can you understand what I'm saying?

David   Kharasho.

Ludmila   He understands like a dog does. But he can't speak. Eat up . . .

Tanya   I'm glad I bought a return ticket. The devil at my shoulder kept whispering: get a return ticket. So I did, cheaper too. Thank God.

David   Kharasho.

Tanya   Dima, I've nothing for you. Let's exchange something. Your sailor's jacket with the shiny buttons, and I'll give you . . . my coat. It's snakeskin, you'll be warm when you play the violin in the underpass . . . I'll wear your jacket, arrive in it in America, take it off and hang it on a hanger. At night I'll stroke it, put my arms around the empty sleeves, look at the left side of the jacket, there where your heart was, and think, yes, someone on this earth does love me, but no matter how much I want to cling to him between us lies an ocean . . . Oh, to cling to you, my invented you in my invented world, in my invented Moscow, my invented Russia . . . The goose has gone. Flown away. Before I forget, here's the key to the flat, take it, Dima, I won't need it now. Poor goose, flying across the ocean to somewhere warm. Birds fly south in the winter. 'Birds of passage in the autumn's blue, to distant lands they fly. Not I, I stay with you!' . . . I learned that at school . . . 'Not I, I stay with you' . . .

Ludmila   Yes, yes! 'Land of my birth, I stay with you! I need no Turkish beaches! I need no foreign soil!' (*Weeps.*) Forgive us, my poor dear, forgive us!

Tanya   For what?

Ludmila   Just forgive us . . .

Tanya (*smiles*)   Just? Very well. And you forgive me. I shall always think of this city now as a huge communal flat, without streets, without paths . . . a communal flat in which there lives a goose, there's a cuckoo on the wall and little lights flicker and the walls are covered with vodka labels, and in this city sirens wail because everywhere fires rage, every second someone dies, in this city people have outbursts of passion, have fits, and in this huge madhouse lives a madman, he stands on a heap of paper, this madman, he only has one eye and he wears a sailor's jacket with bright buttons, there he stands and on his violin he plays 'The Oginski Polonaise, A Farewell to Russia' . . . Excuse me. I must say goodbye to the rooms.

Ludmila   He'll be here soon. There's a double feature today.

Tanya   Who?

Ludmila   Ivan. Indian films, they always come in two parts. 'Ashes and Diamonds', 'Love and Roses' . . . You'd better eat, Tanyechka, that's fat, carbohydrate . . .

Tanya Mila, you don't look like you worry about your health. But I do. I'll need to fly to the Bahamas for a few days, to rest and calm down.

Ludmila I'll say goodbye to Ivan for you, Tanyechka. I'll kiss him goodbye for you. A pity I rushed it and ordered the taxi for nine. It could have come later, only your plane leaves in the night . . .

Tanya The Bahamas, yes. Palm trees, the sun, beautiful people, carefree . . . If I'd been born on the Bahamas I'd have been a Bahamian and father would have been a Bahamian. I'd spend my life under a palm tree holding a candle, and eat nothing but bananas and drink only pineapple juice . . . I'm going to say goodbye to the rooms, I'll put on the jacket. Excuse me.

Ludmila Of course. Go on. As for you, Sergei, either go to the toilet or eat up. Like it?

Sergei I could eat a horse.

Ludmila Well, eat up then.

Tanya *goes into the corridor. Goes into* **Ivan**'*s room. Stands in the centre of it, looks at the walls.*

Ludmila You too, David, eat up. Look at our little foreigner shovelling in his Russian soup. Only don't choke . . .

David Da, da. Pidaras. Pisdya.

Ludmila (*to* **Sergei**) Taught him that, did you? Well done, Sergei! He'll catch on soon . . . Swearing is what you learn in Moscow. Not much else you learn in Moscow, except filth, and that in no time at all.

Tanya (*walking round* **Ivan**'*s room*) Good night, good night, good night, dear friends . . .' (*Calls softly.*) Dima! Come here a minute!

Dima *goes into the corridor, stands in the doorway to* **Ivan**'*s room.*

Ivan'*s room.*

Tanya Dima, I'm so frightened when those cars with the sirens drive past. I keep thinking it's an ambulance come to

take me to a mental hospital on orders from the KGB. Tell me
the truth, look me in the eyes, did she really phone for a taxi?

Dima   Yes.

Tanya   You're lying. You want to send me to an asylum.

Dima   You need treatment.

Tanya (*is silent*)   Give me a cigarette . . .

Dima   Take the pack. A souvenir.

Tanya (*takes the pack, turns it, sits on the floor under the palm*)   The
pack with the fourteen . . . It's cosy here. So this is where he sits
and dreams . . . Look, pictures on the wall, a film – some
pictures, some films won't let me go – they slowly appear and
then just as slowly they fade, they get under my skin, make me
aware, touch my heart, and when I've understood a picture
and taken it all in, all the colours, the sounds, it disappears
and a new picture comes: some in a dream, others when I'm
awake, beautiful, kitschy, an Indian film, nice . . . I look at
your black eye patch and suddenly I'm thinking of the thin
black moustache on the upper lip of a salesman, over there, on
East Street – I'm going down the street in shorts, a red bag
over my shoulder, four children come running up to me,
they're wearing black linen, they see me, look in amazement
at my white skin and their eyes grow big as balloons, they look
at me – one little boy looks with piercing dark eyes and
suddenly it seems as if I'm not me, but that child – and
somewhere in the street there's a crack – no, not a crack, but a
little side street that leads to my home, to my world, to my life,
that's what the crack is: a door out of tin and wood and behind
that door live my mother, my sisters and my brothers, I live
there, and I'm running home, I open the creaking door, there
in a corner lie the toys I've made myself, old and dirty and
dusty, this is my dusty and thorny world, and over a fire in the
middle of the room stands my mother and prepares the
dinner, I sit in the corner, I pick up my toys and wait for the
meal, I want to eat, I rock my straw doll to sleep, I sit and I
know soon my father will come to me from his store, he'll
come for a meal, and the store's opposite our house, my father

sits down angrily, counts money and scowls, next to the shop
on a baking tray or on something made of iron there are
burning coals, and over this iron stands a workman, dirty,
hammering, making jewellery, some kind of long oriental
earrings or bracelets, he does this unskilfully and the sweat
runs down his face, but soon he'll be home, he's thinking of
home and that soon the day will end and the light fade, he
makes jewellery and gives it to the children and the children
sell it to stupid tourists ... (*Pause*.) It took long to tell it, but
these films, these pictures fly past in a second like thousands of
others, I see everything and I feel how alive everything is ...
Your hands, Dimochka, your hands ... You have such
beautiful hands, I've been wanting to tell you for a long time,
so beautiful, I look at them and I think of you playing the
violin in the underpass and how one day I came to in the
underground, I hate the underground, but one day for some
reason I found myself there, how did I get there? It was night,
in front of me, around me tiles, then I heard a trumpet, a
trumpet, I thought, I'm in heaven, but around me was hell.
Why was I in the underground, the trumpet sounded,
heaven, I thought, angels, archangels are singing, but it was
'Tulips in Amsterdam'. Do you remember ... Ta-ri-ra-ri ... I
looked around, why was I here, where was the trumpet?
There was a black musician, it was late at night, he was
playing for the people passing by, wanted alms, or perhaps he
was playing just for himself because he had nowhere to
rehearse and he didn't need charity, there was no need to give
him anything, he was giving to us – music, his music, and
drops of sweat ran down his black, shiny forehead into his ear
and down over his puckered lips and onto the collar of his
white shirt, ruined in the wash ... he was soaked through,
poor man, he had nowhere to play, no home, all he had was
the trumpet and a black bag wide open at his feet and the bag
was begging for alms, begging for itself not for its owner: he
needs nothing, he's in heaven, all he needs is air – to breathe in
and out and send his music into the world, that underpass isn't
his world, music is: notes that build a house, build streets,
music that weaves a heaven, the sun, people that sing, not
talk, all sculpted in music ... A trumpet in the underground,

polished till it blazes – not a soul, only rats, rats somewhere in the darkness, scurrying and hearing the music – Forgive me, Dimochka, I'm to blame for everything, I didn't take you seriously, I thought it was all a joke, I didn't believe and now you don't love me, you only pity me – Well, that's all right, that's how it is, in America I'll know that someone thinks of me and pities me . . .

Ivan *comes into the corridor and then goes into his room.*

Ivan   Hello.

Tanya   Oh, excuse me, Ivan, I'm in your room, I'm disturbing you . . . I wanted to say goodbye . . . Excuse me. And goodbye. Goodbye. You're a sweet man . . .

Is silent, looks at **Ivan**.
Ivan *lowers his eyes, grows uneasy.*

Ivan   What's the matter? . . . This is like a funeral . . . As if someone had just died . . . What? . . . You're no stranger at this festival of life, not you . . . Wait . . .

Runs to the pot with the palm, digs in it, gets out a tin, the money, hands it to **Tanya**.

Here. Take it, Tatyana Danilovna . . . It's yours. You'll need it over there. Take it, take it, I don't need it . . .

Tanya, *bewildered, stands holding the money.*

Tanya   Thank you, Vanya . . . But I'm sure you need it yourself, take it . . .

Ivan (*frightened, rejects it*)   Oh, whatever next, really! What for! I'm not Kaltenbrunner or Schnitzelbaum or Barenboim! You need it. Take it. Take it!

He bursts into tears, kisses **Tanya**, *sits down under the palm.*
Tanya *is silent.*

Tanya   These Russians are unpredictable. I'm not used to it any more. I don't know what to say. One minute they hate you, then it's love, and then it's something else again . . . Thank you, Vanya. You're a good man. Thank you . . .

Ivan (*crying*)   Go, go! I cry as it is, go! You need it more. Live your life. It'll be hard for you in America! We'll get by here. Both of you, go!

Tanya   Goodbye, Vanya. (*Looks round the room.*) Thank you. All my life I've depended on the kindness of strangers . . . I read that somewhere . . . Goodbye.

Goes out into the corridor. Takes the sailor's jacket from the stand. Slowly, as if putting on a skin, she tries it on, puts her arms in the sleeves.

Is silent.

Sits on her case.

Dima *stands in the doorway of* **Ivan**'s *room, his head against the door frame, and smokes.*

The corridor.

Tanya   Goodbye, goodbye, goodbye . . . Goodbye-goodbye-goodbye . . . Goodbye, goodbye, goodbye, goodbye, goodbye, goodbye . . . 'Moscow, how much that word means, how it echoes in a Russian heart!' . . . Goodbye, goodbye, goodbye, goodbye . . . 'No foe shall ever make thee bow thy head! Oh Moscow, golden Moscow mine, my heart lies at thy feet! . . . Goodbye, goodbye, goodbye, goodbye, goodbye, goodbye . . .

Ludmila *and* **Sergei** *come from the kitchen, stop, look at* **Tanya**. **David** *sits eating in the kitchen.*

Tanya (*mutters*)   Goodbye, goodbye, goodbye . . . Goodbye-goodbye-goodbye . . . 'Oh my country, let me declare my love, hear it one more time.' . . . Goodbye . . . Goodnight, dear friends . . .

Gets up from the case, carefully opens the door to **Dima**'s *room. Goes into the darkness, stands in the centre of the room.*

Dima's *room.*

Aunt Lydia is sitting on a chair by the window, knitting. She raises her head, looks at **Tanya** *from under her glasses, smiles. Is silent and tense.*

Goodbye, Aunty Lydia . . . Goodbye. (*Sings softly.*) 'Blue the nights, camp fires blaze; the children of workers, pioneers we!

For us a new age dawns bright. Be prepared! we cry. Be
prepared!' (*Pause.*) Goodbye.

Goes into the corridor. Then into **Ludmila** *and* **Sergei**'s *room.*

(*Mutters.*) Witch's whiskers, devil's toe, little monkey, go go
go! Hop, skip, you're it!

Ludmila *and* **Sergei**'s *room.*

*Her father and mother sit in different corners of the room. Look with a
smile at* **Tanya**.

Goodbye, goodbye, goodbye. Goodbye, mother, goodbye,
father. Goodbye. Goodbye. (*Is silent.*) 'Day by day the years
go by, new generations rise, unforgotten one name lives on –
Lenin! Lenin never dies! Always with me, my grief he shares,
my hope, my joy! Oh Lenin!' (*Pause.*) Goodbye. Good night,
dear friends . . .

Goes into the corridor, carefully closes the door behind her.

The corridor.

Sits on the suitcase. Smiles, looks at **Sergei**, **Ludmila** *and* **Dima**.

That's it. I've said goodbye. Goodbye, all of you. Goodbye,
goodbye, goodbye, goodbye.

Ludmila (*cries*)   Until the next time, my dear. The next
time.

Tanya   We'll wait here for the taxi. It'll be here any minute.
Goodbye, Dimochka. Don't forget me. And I won't forget
you. Visit me in America if you want, if you've the time. I
know you're busy, every day in the underpass on the violin,
the Oginski Polonaise . . . Perhaps I'll come back some day,
then you can play the violin and I'll dance the little swan
beside you . . . (*Smiles.*) Perhaps someone will take pity and
throw us some money . . . (*Loudly.*) David! Time to go!

David *comes out of the kitchen. He goes to the front door, takes the
mirror fragment, looks at himself, puts on lipstick. Sits on the floor by the
case, rests his head against* **Tanya**'s *knees. Sits at her feet like a puppy.*
Tanya *draws* **David** *to her, smiles.* **Ivan** *comes out of his room. All*

stand and look at **Tanya** *sitting on her suitcase and* **David** *at her feet. They are silent.*

Tanya   Dear David! My little boy! My happiness! How I love you! We're going home, David? Domoi. Home . . . Goodbye. We're going home. Domoi . . . domoi . . .

David (*smiles, looks* **Tanya** *in the eyes*)   Domoi . . . We're going home . . . Goodbye . . . Domoi . . . Domoi . . .

Tanya   Goodbye, goodbye, goodbye, goodbye, goodbye, goodbye, goodbye.

All look at **Tanya** *and* **David** *in silence.*

Ivan   Poor woman . . . so far away . . . why . . .

Sergei   That's how it is, they don't sleep together, but somehow they have children . . . Goodbye.

Dima   Goodbye.

Ludmila (*wipes away her tears*)   Never mind . . . the taxi'll be here in a minute . . . Don't worry . . . It'll all turn out all right . . . Not all right here though, but in Ulan Ude, that's where we'll go, to my daughter – they've got a different meridian there . . . Never mind. We'll survive. We're unsinkable . . .

Tanya *sits on the suitcase, her back straight,* **David** *at her feet.*

It grows darker.

Sirens outside.

Aunt Lydia, the father and mother come into the room, look at **Tanya**.

Outside the window, rising above the sirens comes the sound of an orchestra playing a festive, but somehwhat sad march based on the Oginski Polonaise.

Darkness.

New titles also available from Methuen

John Godber
Lucky Sods & Passion Killers
0 413 70170 0

Paul Godfrey
A Bucket of Eels & The Modern Husband
0 413 68830 5

Jonathan Harvey
Boom Bang-A-Bang & Rupert Street Lonely Hearts Club
0 413 70450 5

Phyllis Nagy
Weldon Rising & Disappeared
0 413 70150 6

Judy Upton
Bruises & The Shorewatchers' House
0 413 70430 0